I0448188

TABLE OF CONTENTS

INTRODUCTION

The concept of deterrence is as old as war, but deterrence theory and strategy came to the forefront of strategic thought with the advent of nuclear weapons. Recently, the Capstone Concept for Joint Operations identified deterring potential adversaries as one of five broad national security challenges. The document further identified "developing better ways to measure the effectiveness of deterrence efforts is a vital requirement."[1] If deterrence effectiveness is held in the minds of the adversary and the adversary will not readily admit to being deterred, how can leaders and planners determine if deterrence messages have been received and properly interpreted? This paper proposes that planners can develop alternative measures of effectiveness for deterrence activities and messages. Properly developed priority intelligence requirements can assist planners in determining if deterrence operations are achieving the desired end states.

Military operations alone do not deter aggression; deterrence strategies must integrate and synchronize all elements of national power, which include diplomatic, information, military and economic. For the purpose of this paper, research and analysis will focus on military activities that support national deterrence policy and strategy as well as the environment and indicators prevalent prior to military deterrence activities.

Deterrence theories and strategies have evolved since the detonation of nuclear weapons in 1945. Chapter 1 will define terms and processes used for developing this paper starting with the definition of deterrence as "the prevention from action by fear of consequences. Deterrence is a state of mind brought about by existence of a credible

---

[1] U.S. Joint Chiefs of Staff, *Capstone Concept for Joint Operations* (Washington DC: Government Printing Office, January 2009), 9-10.

threat of unacceptable counteraction."[2] This chapter further discusses two methods used to deter adversary aggression through denial and punishment, the difference between general and immediate deterrence and whether the focus of deterrence is central or extended. Furthermore, a discussion of deterrent options and flexible deterrent options will show the supporting relationship between dissuasion and deterrence operations.

After defining the scope of deterrence, Chapter 1 highlights the importance of feedback during the communication process and the challenges associated with obtaining this feedback from deterrence activities and messages. Finally, this chapter defines measure of effectiveness as "a criterion used to assess changes in system behavior, capability, or operational environment that is tied to measuring the attainment of an end state, achievement of an objective, or creation of an effect."[3] It also provides a brief summary of the challenges of studying deterrence measures of effectiveness.

Before planners can develop deterrence measures of effectiveness, they must first study doctrine and understand current deterrence strategy desired end states. Chapter 2 will first document the search for guiding principles contained in deterrence doctrine. While service level nuclear deterrence doctrine exists, joint deterrence doctrine does not exist. In place of doctrine, this chapter will review guidance contained in the Deterrence Operations Joint Operating Concept dated 2006 followed by a review of how strategic deterrence strategy evolved. Using the insights gained, a review of current deterrence strategies will reveal that deterrence strategies generally remain unchanged.

A review of national, departmental and combatant commander level strategies will disclose the United States continues to develop and publicize general deterrence

---

[2] U.S. Joint Chiefs of Staff, *Joint Publication 1-02: Department of Defense Dictionary of Military and Associated Terms* (Washington DC: Government Printing Office, September 2010), 135.
[3] Ibid., 289.

strategies. These strategies focus on global and regional audiences and do not focus on specific adversary decision makers. This makes measuring the effects of deterrence operations difficult. Additionally, U.S. deterrence strategies do not incorporate the limited guidance contained in the Deterrence Operations Joint Operating Concept.

Chapter 3 will use the principles of deterrence operations to examine four historical diplomatic dissuasion and military deterrence cases. The four cases will highlight that events and activities provided indicators that dissuasion and deterrence efforts were failing. The first case will examine U.S. attempts to dissuade Japan from continued aggression at the beginning of World War II and deterrence activities and messages towards the end of World War II. Next, events leading up to the Cuban Missile Crisis will highlight both the initial deterrence failures and ultimately the deterrence success. The events that influenced Libyan leaders to change their policy from supporting terrorism and pursuing weapons of mass destruction (WMD) to renouncing terrorism and countering WMD proliferation is the third case to be examined. The last historical case examined reviews the events and activities designed to influence Iraqi leaders prior to Gulf War I. In addition to the four case studies, a few examples of military flexible deterrent options that support strategic deterrence strategy will be examined.

In the absence of non-nuclear deterrence doctrine, planners can review similar doctrine and historical events to document and apply lessons learned in developing deterrence plans. Chapter 4 will review and highlight principles contained in the Joint Doctrine for Military Deception. Many military deception principles have relevance to deterrence operations since both types of operations attempt to influence the mind of the adversary decision maker to take an action or inaction favorable to U.S. objectives. This chapter will examine three military deception operations, specifically Operation MINCEMEAT, Operation CAMILLA and Operation STARKEY. The associated feedback and varying degrees of success will be analyzed. The chapter will conclude with recommendations for applying the lessons learned from military deception operations to future deterrence operations.

Chapter 5 will examine conclusions derived from four studies of why deterrence succeeded or failed. Combining these conclusions with indications from the historical cases in Chapter 4, this paper will propose a list of indicators. Planners can use the indicators to develop alternative measures of effectiveness. The indicators are grouped into six categories: political indicators, alliances, economic considerations, understanding motivation, communication and military forces. Planners can use the list to develop priority intelligence requirements and obtain indirect feedback from deterrence operatons. In the historical cases, adversary statements and military activities provided evidence that general deterrence efforts failed. In the cases of the Cuban Missile Crisis and Libya, a change in deterrence strategy can also change the adversary's course of action and lead to success.

Chapter 6 provides recommendations to improve U.S. deterrence efforts. To develop better measures of effectiveness, Joint Staff must develop deterrence doctrine and leaders must develop better deterrence strategies. A third recommendation creates an implementing arm to integrate and synchronize deterrence activities and messages across all U.S. Government Departments. Finally, Chapter 6 recommends planners use the list of deterrence indicators to use to develop PIRs for analyzing deterrence activities and messages effectiveness.

This paper will conclude that while the adversary will not readily admit to being deterred or not deterred, intelligence indicators provide feedback to the potential effectiveness, or ineffectiveness, of deterrence activities and messages. Examining the political indicators, economic considerations, communications and military forces along with understanding alliances and adversary motivations provides feedback as to how the adversary decision makers will respond to U.S. deterrence activities. U.S. leadership must resist using their own preconceptions in order to determine the adversary's reaction and adjust the United States' approach when required to deter adversaries from taking an undesired action.

CHAPTER 1
DEFINING THE TERMS

Deterrence theory and strategy have evolved since the employment of nuclear weapons in 1945. Nations have developed various deterrence strategies and used a variety of ways to implement, communicate, and measure deterrence operations. In order to ensure a common understanding of deterrence for this paper, this chapter will define deterrence and include the commonly accepted methods, categories, focus and options used to implement deterrence operations. Additionally, a review of the communication process will highlight the challenges with obtaining feedback from deterrence activities. Finally, this chapter will define measures of effectiveness and provide a brief overview of the challenges associated with measuring the effectiveness of deterrence operations.

Deterrence

Under Sun Tzu's offensive strategy he stated, "those skilled in war subdue the enemy's army without battle."[1] This in essence is the ultimate objective of deterrence. Joint Publication 1-02 defines deterrence as "the prevention from action by fear of consequences. Deterrence is a state of mind brought about by existence of a credible threat of unacceptable counteraction."[2] In other words, U.S. deterrence strategy should influence the adversary's decision makers to believe that the costs the United States will impose for aggression will exceed any benefits or gains the adversary perceives.

Deterrence Methods: Deterrence strategies employ two common methods to deter potential adversaries. The first method is deterrence by denial. Defensive capabilities

---

[1] Sun Tzu, *The Art of War,* trans. Samuel B. Griffith (New York: Oxford University Press, 1971), 79.
[2] U.S. Joint Chiefs of Staff, *Joint Publication 1-02*, 135.

deny the adversary benefits of a successful attack or offensive capabilities deny the adversary any potential gain. Military forces employ defensive measures, such as ground based intercept missiles designed to defeat adversary missile attacks and offensive capabilities, such as survivable retaliatory strike weapons to deny any potential gains. These capabilities intend to influence the adversary's cost benefit analysis into believing that any perceived benefits are unlikely to be gained.

The second method is deterrence by punishment. The majority of military deterrence activities focus on deterrence by punishment. This method convinces the adversary decision maker that the defending nation will respond and impose severe costs associated with adversary aggression. The adversary must believe that the costs associated with a retaliatory strike outweigh any perceived beneficial gain.

Other deterrence theories associate deterrence denial and punishment methods with the methods of encouraging adversary restraint and compelling the adversary to action or inaction. While these methods mutually support deterrence strategies, they do not meet the definition of deterrence since they do not use fear of consequence to influence the adversary decision maker. Instead, these methods use pressure negotiations to convince the adversary there are benefits to restraint or the desired action.

Deterrence Categories: In 1983, Patrick Morgan categorized the practice of deterrence into two categories: general and immediate.[3] General deterrence consists of a nation maintaining a formidable military capability and publicizing its commitment to deny benefits and impose punishment in response to aggression from another nation. Nations direct general deterrence messages for global audiences to consider and not to a specific nation.

---

[3] Patrick Morgan, *Deterrence Now* (Cambridge: Cambridge University Press, 2003), 9.

When a nation perceives an unacceptable threat, then general deterrence has failed and the nation will take immediate deterrence actions. Immediate deterrence encompasses conveying a punitive threat to an opposing nation when one perceives that the opponent is posturing to attack and/or war is imminent.

Deterrence Focus: Nations can focus their deterrence activities centrally or extend them to third party nations. A central deterrence focus relates to deterring attacks against a nation's sovereign territories or against its vital interest. Extended deterrence occurs when a nation threatens to retaliate on behalf of a third party nation with or without a formal agreement.

Deterrent Options: Effective deterrence operations must integrate and synchronize all elements of national power, which include diplomatic, information, military and economic. Joint doctrine defines deterrent options as "a course of action, developed on the best economic, diplomatic, political and military judgment, designed to dissuade an adversary from a current course of action or contemplated operations."[4]

Flexible Deterrent Option: "The flexible deterrent option is the means by which the various diplomatic, information, military, and economic deterrent measures available to the President are included in the joint operation planning process."[5] A nation executes military and nonmilitary flexible deterrent options to resolve an issue without conflict or deter further aggression during crisis situations. See Appendix 1 for examples of flexible deterrent options for each instrument of national power.

---

[4] U.S. Joint Chiefs of Staff, *Joint Publication 1-02*, 135.
[5] Ibid., 177.

Communicating Deterrence Strategy

Deterrence strategy requires more than maintaining the capability to deny or punish the adversary; nations must communicate it. Whether it is general or immediate deterrence, central or extended, nations must send unambiguous and credible deterrence messages.[6] They can communicate their deterrence messages directly or indirectly using multiple combinations of written, verbal and visual information channels. Direct channels include, but are not limited to, presidential and diplomatic communiqués and United Nations Resolutions. Indirect channels include public statements such as Presidential speeches, written documents like the National Security Strategy and military activities such as military posturing and show of force demonstrations.

The communication process is the inter-relationship between the sender, the message, the receiver and the receiver's interpretation of the message in the form of feedback. All four parts are essential to effective communication, but the most important part is feedback to ensure the receiver received the message and the receiver properly understood it. Unfortunately, when it comes to being deterred, generally the intended recipient will not provide direct feedback. The fact that the intended receiver may misinterpret the message due to differences in culture and thought compounds the problem with the deterrence communication process. Furthermore, when communicating indirect deterrence messages, sometimes the intended recipient does not receive the message. Therefore, due to the lack of direct feedback and the possibility of misinterpretation and failed receipt, planners must develop alternative ways to measure deterrence effectiveness through indirect feedback.

---

[6] Richard Lebow and Janice Stein, *When Does Deterrence Succeed and How Do We Know?* (Ottawa: Canadian Institute for International Peace and Security, 1990), 60.

Deterrence Measures of Effectiveness

Joint doctrine defines measures of effectiveness (MOE) as "a criterion used to assess changes in system behavior, capability, or operational environment that is tied to measuring the attainment of an end state, achievement of an objective, or creation of an effect."[7] Measurements allow leaders to determine if the deterrence messages created the desired effect. However, Henry Kissinger accurately described the challenges with measuring deterrence effectiveness when he wrote, "Since deterrence can only be tested negatively, by events that do not take place, and since it is never possible to demonstrate why something has *not* occurred, it became especially difficult to assess whether the existing policy was the best possible policy or just a barely effective one."[8]

Many scholars have conducted studies to analyze the efficiency of deterrence policy and strategy. These studies attempted to determine when and why deterrence succeeded or failed with widely mixed results. The studies used different definitions and criteria for analyzing deterrence successes and failures; therefore comparing the results of the studies is difficult. However, the case studies disclosed various intelligence indicators that revealed deterrence efforts were failing. The indicators provided indirect feedback that deterrence activities had or had not influenced the adversary decision maker from taking or preparing to take the undesired action. By analyzing these studies and drawing out common indicators, planners can use indirect feedback to develop alternative measures of effectiveness. Over time, proper intelligence indicator analysis can determine if the desired effect and deterrence objective are being achieved.

---

[7] U.S. Joint Chiefs of Staff, *Joint Publication 1-02*, 289.
[8] Henry Kissinger, *Diplomacy* (New York: Simon and Schuster, 1994), 608.

CHAPTER 2
DETERRENCE DOCTRINE AND STRATEGY

Nations develop doctrine and strategy for employing the instruments of national power in a synchronized and integrated fashion to achieve national objectives.[1] Before planners develop measures of effectiveness (MOE), they should turn to doctrine for guiding principles in executing deterrence operations. In the absence of formal doctrine, planners can use the observations they draw from history to develop guiding principles to examine current strategy. Planners review strategy to understand the desired end states and objectives. Utilizing this understanding, they can develop MOEs.

This Chapter begins by documenting that deterrence doctrine does not exist but the United States Strategic Command's Deterrence Operations Joint Operating Concept (DO JOC) contains limited deterrence operations guidance. In the absence of doctrine, this chapter will review U.S. deterrence strategy evolution to provide fundamental principles to consider when examining deterrence strategy. Using the DO JOC guidance and the fundamental principles, a review of national, departmental and combatant commander level strategy documents will be conducted. This examination will reveal that the United States publicizes a general deterrence strategy that is difficult to measure. Additionally, the United States struggles with integrating and synchronizing deterrence efforts across different departments.

---

[1] U.S. Joint Chiefs of Staff, *Joint Publication 3-0: Joint Operations,* Change 2 (Washington DC: Government Printing Office, March 2010), I-3.

Deterrence Doctrine

Doctrine provides guiding principles for executing operations. A search for joint deterrence doctrine disclosed that joint deterrence doctrine does not exist.[2] However, United States Strategic Command published the DO JOC in 2006 which provides guidance to joint force commanders on how to conduct deterrence operations eight to twenty years into the future. "The central idea of the DO JOC is to decisively influence the adversary's decision-making calculus in order to prevent hostile actions against US vital interests."[3]

The DO JOC identifies denying benefits, imposing costs and encouraging adversary restraint as the three ways to achieve deterrence. Denying benefits and imposing costs are similar to denial and punishment methods previously identified in Chapter 1. While the tenet "encouraging adversary restraint" supports deterrence operations, this method does not meet the joint definition of deterrence. Deterrence prevents actions through fear of consequences; encouraging adversary restraint uses pressure negotiations to convince the adversary that there are benefits to not taking the action the United States seeks to deter.[4] The responsibility for these negotiations resides primarily with the Department of State; therefore, the DO JOC should address how military operations support Department of State initiatives.

---

[2] U.S. Joint Chiefs of Staff, *Joint Doctrine, Education, & Training Electronic Information System, Joint Publications, Index,* https://jdeis.js.mil/jdeis/index.jsp?pindex=2 (accessed April 4, 2011). The U.S. Air Force Doctrine Document 3-72: Nuclear Operations and the Naval Operations Concept 2010 documents focus on providing trained and equipped nuclear forces to create a credible deterrent capability for political leaders to employ should the need arise. They primarily focus on nuclear surety and positive control concepts to ensure safe, secure and reliable operations but do not focus on employment strategies.
[3] Commander, U.S. Strategic Command, *Deterrence Operations Joint Operating Concept Version 2.0.* (Omaha: United States Strategic Command, December, 2006), 5.
[4] Ibid., 28.

After providing the methods, the DO JOC discusses various military means and how they contribute to deterrence operations. The means included are global situational awareness, command and control, forward presence, security cooperation, force projection, active and passive defenses, global strike and strategic communications. While the DO JOC does not provide doctrinal guidance for each mean, it provides the joint force commander ways to consider employing each capability.

The DO JOC recognizes that planners must integrate deterrence operations into military planning and provides five steps to implement deterrence operations. The first step directs planners to specify the deterrence objectives. They must clearly identify who is being deterred, what action the adversary is being deterred from taking and under what conditions. When developing the objective, planners must consider the impact of third-party contributions and mitigate risks with competing objectives.

During step two, planners assess the decision calculus of adversary decision-makers. This requires in-depth intelligence analysis of factors that influence the adversary decision maker's cost benefit analysis, how the adversary decision maker perceives the costs, benefits and consequences and any uncertainties associated with the assessment.

In step three, planners identify the desired effects deterrence operations should have on the adversary's decision calculus. Associated with the desired effects, the DO JOC states that planners should develop MOEs for the desired effects but does not provide guidance on how to develop the MOEs.

Step four is to develop and assess tailored courses of action designed to achieve the desired deterrence effects. The course of action should decisively influence the adversary to believe that the United States will deny them the benefits they seek, play upon their fears and present them with alternatives to encourage restraint. Finally, the last step directs planners to monitor and assess the adversary's response to the executed course of action.

In the absence of deterrence doctrine, the next section will provide a summary of how deterrence strategy evolved and document guiding principles that can supplement the guidance contained in the DO JOC. The summary begins with historical deterrence strategy before the detonation of nuclear weapons, discusses the impact nuclear weapons had on Truman's, Eisenhower's, Kennedy's and Johnson's Administrations deterrence strategies and the associated outcomes.

Deterrence Strategy Evolution

Throughout history, military operations have supported deterrence strategies. Thucydides recorded the use of maneuvers to influence the opponent into thinking that beginning or expanding a war was not worth the risks or perceived costs.[5] Deterrence strategy focused on developing and maintaining military capabilities or a perceived capability such that in case of an attack, a nation could retaliate and win. Furthermore, weaker nations aligned with other nations to balance their power against stronger nations to avoid coercion. While developing and employing new weapons changed the military's tactics, techniques and procedures for fighting wars, the ultimate objective to create a fear of punishment in order to deter adversary aggression did not change.

The development and employment of nuclear weapons in 1945 changed the U.S. leadership's focus of warfare from one of winning wars to one of averting wars.[6] The

---

[5] George and Smoke, *Deterrence in American Foreign Policy: Theory and Practice* (New York: Columbia University Press, 1974), 12.
[6] Bernard Brodie, ed., *The Absolute Weapon: Atomic Power and World Order* (New York: Harcourt, Brace and Company, 1946), 76.

14

new strategy focused on the destructive capability of nuclear weapons, rather than on the credible employment of these weapons, to create the fear of consequence. At the conclusion of World War II, the Truman Administration focused on demobilizing the large wartime force structure and viewed nuclear weapons as a relatively low cost means to deter aggression. Leaders assumed that the threat created by having nuclear weapons would deter adversaries from attacking the United States, its interests or its allies unless the aggressor accepted the risk of nuclear retaliation. The Truman Administration failed to consider that adversaries seeking limited objectives did not perceive a U.S. nuclear response as a credible threat. As a result of the adversary's perceptions, nuclear weapons did not deter the North Korean invasion of South Korea or the Soviet Union's Blockade of Berlin.

The Eisenhower Administration's "New Look" studied the ineffectiveness of nuclear weapons to deter communist aggression and publicized a new policy. In his January 1954 speech, Secretary of State John Dulles outlined that the United States had adopted a policy of massive retaliation which would include the immediate use of nuclear weapons in response to any aggression.[7] However, massive retaliation began to lose credibility in the late 1950s as the Soviet Union's nuclear arsenal grew. The fact that the United States did not use nuclear weapons to respond to the Berlin crisis in 1958 compounded the problem. If the adversary does not view the deterrence threat as credible, the deterrence strategy will not be effective. The time when nuclear weapons alone provided the basis for deterrence had ended.

In 1961, the Kennedy Administration believed a strong conventional force and a flexible response strategy backed by nuclear weapons would deter aggression. This

---

[7] George and Smoke, 27.

strategy accounted for not using nuclear weapons during limited conflicts such as the Vietnam War. During this same timeframe, the Soviet Union publicly claimed that their nuclear capabilities met or exceeded the capabilities of the United States. Their claims created a perceived missile gap and played upon the fears of the American public who in turn demanded increased defense spending. Planners focused on the adversary's capabilities, rather than on the adversary's intentions, creating the nuclear arms race.[8] As the arms race continued, the Johnson Administration adopted a mutual assured destruction strategy. Leaders believed that maintaining an arsenal of nuclear weapons large enough to unmistakably inflict unacceptable damage on an aggressor even after absorbing a first strike would deter aggression.[9]

The United States also extended its deterrence strategy through formal agreements and informal support. The United States formalized its commitment to extended deterrence as a signatory to the North Atlantic Treaty. Article 5 of the treaty declares that an armed attack on one nation is considered an attack on all nations and provides for a collective defense.[10] Smaller nations of NATO have used this agreement, along with an assurance that the United States will use nuclear weapons when required, as the foundation for not developing their own nuclear capabilities.

Informally, the United States extended its deterrence capabilities on several occasions. Most notable are U.S. support to South Korea and Taiwan. Another example includes the U.S. show of force demonstrations designed to deter a coup attempt against President

---

[8] Bernard Brodie, ed., *The Future of Deterrence in U.S. Strategy* (Los Angeles: University of California, 1968), 127.
[9] Lawrence Freedman, *The Evolution of Nuclear Strategy* (New York: St. Martin's Press, 1989), 246.
[10] North Atlantic Treaty Organization Secretary General, *NATO Handbook* (Brussels: NATO Public Diplomacy Division, 2006), 372.

Aquino's government. The U.S. military conducted fighter aircraft patrols over rebel

airfields and placed two aircraft carriers off the coast of the Philippines in 1989.[11]

The United States communicated its general deterrence strategies and backed them

with robust conventional and nuclear military capabilities, yet crisis situations developed

requiring immediate deterrence operations to stop or prevent further aggression.

Therefore, deterrence strategies based upon military capabilities alone do not deter; the

strategies must create a credible threat as perceived by the adversary decision maker.

Additionally, deterrence strategies must also consider the adversary's intent and not just

their military capabilities. The next section will review how current deterrence strategy

implements DO JOC guidance and observations from how deterrence strategy has

evolved.

Current Deterrence Strategy

The United States publicizes its general deterrence strategy in a variety of documents

at the national, departmental and combatant commander levels. At the national level, the

National Security Strategy documents the President's deterrence related guidance using a

whole of government approach. Another document, the U.S. National Strategy for Public

Diplomacy and Strategic Communications, developed by the Department of State,

attempts to implement the National Security Strategy guidance and synchronize the

nation's messages across all departments.[12] However, each department develops its own

strategy to implement the President's guidance. The Department of Defense provides

---

[11] U.S. Joint Chiefs of Staff, *Joint Publication 3-0*, VII-8.

[12] U.S. Department of State, Under Secretary for Public Diplomacy and Public Affairs, *U.S. National Strategy for Public Diplomacy and Strategic Communication* (Washington DC: Government Printing Office, May 2007). The National Security Council established a new Policy Coordinating Committee on Public Diplomacy and Strategic Communications in April 2006. The Department of State, Undersecretary for Public Diplomacy and Public Affairs leads the committee that is charged with interagency public diplomacy and strategic communication strategy development.

deterrence strategy and guidance to subordinate commanders using the Quadrennial Defense Review (QDR). Similarly, the Combatant Commanders develop Theater Campaign Plans (TCP) and operations and concept plans to address their assigned mission to deter aggression. These plans support higher level strategies and articulate to subordinate units the Combatant Commander's desired end states and the ways and means to deter aggression.

National Level Strategy: The first strategy document examined is the National Security Strategy which identifies two deterrence related end states: "security of the United States, its citizens, and U.S. allies and partners" and promoting universal values and international order.[13] It outlines using the whole of government approach as a way to achieve security and international order. To achieve this, the strategy states the United States will focus on strengthening the military to deter aggression across a full range of military operations.[14] Furthermore, the United States must have the ability to identify and interdict threats, deny aggressors the ability to operate and punish aggression if required.[15]

The National Security Strategy communicates the U.S. general deterrence strategy to multiple audiences but does not identify specific adversary decision makers to influence. This makes it difficult to measure the effects that strengthening the military and its capabilities have on the adversary's decision making calculus. The strategy also recognizes that military capabilities alone do not deter, but the document does not assign tasks or specify lead agencies for integrating and synchronizing deterrence efforts across

---

[13] Ibid. U.S. President, *National Security Strategy* (Washington DC: Government Printing Office, May 2010), 7.
[14] Ibid., 14.
[15] Ibid., 18.

all departments. Instead, each department develops and implements its own strategy to meet the desired end states contained in the National Security Strategy.

One national strategy document does attempt to synchronize efforts across all departments and supports the National Security Strategy. The Department of State developed the U.S. National Strategy for Public Diplomacy and Strategic Communications document to synchronize U.S. Government strategic communications. This document primarily focuses on public diplomacy efforts underscoring what the people of the United States value; that men and women are equal and have a right to freedom and government by representation. While this document does not specifically address deterrence messages, it guides communicating messages to isolate terrorists and violent extremists, build partnerships to promote peaceful resolutions of conflicts and protect common interests.[16]

The Policy Coordinating Committee on Public Diplomacy and Strategic Communication oversees and coordinates strategic communications concerning violent extremist and terrorist activity. The committee develops and distributes core strategic messages through the Counterterrorism Coordination Center so public affairs personnel can present a unified message across government agencies. The coordination center primarily focuses on strategic messages against violent extremist and terrorist activities; it does not address aggression from other actors. The committee should expand its strategic communications focus to include developing and coordinating messages designed to deter state and non-state actor aggression.

---

[16] U.S. Department of State, Under Secretary for Public Diplomacy and Public Affairs, *Strategy for Public Diplomacy*, 3.

National level strategies are broad in scope and publicize the U.S. general deterrence strategies to a global audience. Since these strategies do not identify specific decision makers to influence, developing measures of effectiveness is difficult. Additionally, mechanisms to integrate and synchronize deterrence operations across all elements of national power require improvement. The next section will review the Secretary of Defense guidance for implementing the strategy contained in the National Security Strategy.

Department Level Strategy: The Quadrennial Defense Review provides Secretary of Defense guidance for implementing the strategy contained in the National Security Strategy. To strengthen the military and its capabilities, the 2010 QDR identifies four priority objectives that support deterrence operations:

- Prevail in today's wars
- Prevent and deter conflict
- Prepare to defeat adversaries and succeed in a wide range of contingencies
- Preserve and enhance the All-volunteer Force[17]

Under prevail in today's wars, the United States will continue to support the governments of Iraq and Afghanistan to eliminate safe havens and deter support to Al Qaeda. Preventing conflict requires employing all instruments of national power; however, the Department of Defense must strengthen interagency partnerships, starting with the Department of State, the intelligence community and Department of Homeland Security, to improve deterrence operations unity of effort. Deterring conflict requires a capable all-volunteer military force able to fight limited and full scale wars in air, land, sea, space and cyber domains located in Europe, the Pacific, the Greater Middle East, Africa and the

---

[17] U.S. Department of Defense, *Quadrennial Defense Review Report* (Washington DC: Government Printing Office, February 2010), v.

Western Hemisphere. The military must maintain the ability to defeat state and non-state actor aggression against U.S. vital interests.[18]

Similar to the National Security Strategy, the QDR is a general deterrence strategy intended for a wide audience and does not specify individual decision makers. However, the QDR does categorize the audiences by region and provides broad deterrence objectives for each. This strategy also identifies the requirement for an improved planning process to best employ all instruments of national power and improve planning, analysis and assessments. These assessments should measure the effectiveness of employing all instruments of power in preventing conflict and the effectiveness of military force capabilities to deter conflict and defeat state and non-state actor aggression.

Combatant Command Level Strategies: To transition from national and departmental level general deterrence strategy to deterrence operations, the Unified Command Plan tasks each Geographic Combatant Commander (GCC), Commander United States Special Operations Command and Commander United States Strategic Command with "detecting, deterring, and preventing attacks against the United States, its territories, possessions, and bases, and employing appropriate force to defend the nation should deterrence fail."[19] Additionally, the Commander United States Strategic Command has lead responsibility for planning and executing strategic deterrence operations. This includes deterrence by denial with missile defense and second strike capabilities, as well as, deterrence by punishment using global strike capabilities including kinetic, non-kinetic, conventional and nuclear capabilities.[20]

---

[18] Ibid., vi.
[19] U.S. Joint Chiefs of Staff, *Unified Command Plan* (Washington DC: Government Printing Office, April 2011), 6. The same verbiage is found on pages 8, 10, 12, 16, 19, 25 and 28.
[20] Ibid., 28-31.

The GCCs direct their staffs to develop Theater Campaign Plans (TCP), concept plans and operation plans to implement the tasks contained in the Unified Command Plan. The TCP executes the GCC's overarching theater strategy focusing on detecting, deterring and preventing attacks. The concept plans and operation plans employ military forces should deterrence fail. A review of combatant commander level strategies follows, starting with examining the TCPs.

Planners design the TCPs so that military activities shape the regional environment in which military forces must operate. Deterrence activities within the TCPs focus on influencing state and non-state actors within the geographic region. Military operations directed by these plans intend to deter attacks against U.S. interests through a U.S. forward basing presence, enhanced security cooperation and regional partnership building. TCPs also contain an annex for interagency coordination; optimally, planners closely coordinate TCP activities with Department of State, embassy and other U.S. Government personnel to ensure synchronized messages and activities.

Overall, the TCP articulates the Combatant Commander's desired steady state operations required to achieve national and regional objectives. TCPs attempt to influence state and non-state actors, but the majority of TCPs do not identify specific decision makers to influence. These plans also promote the whole of government approach; however, a Combatant Commander may have up to fifty-three Ambassadors and country teams to coordinate with in addition to other U.S. Government agencies.[21] This makes true synchronization difficult. The ultimate goal is to deter and prevent

---

[21] Ibid., TAB. The Commander, U.S. AFRICOM (CDRUSAFRICOM) has the largest number of countries assigned to his area of responsibility. CDRUSAFRICOM is responsible for military activities within 53 nations while the other Combatant Commanders have less. Department of State diplomatic relations within the 53 nations may require the appointment of an Ambassador and country teams.

conflict while at the same time prepare for decisive military operations should a crisis occur.

Combatant Commanders direct development of concept plans or operation plans to prepare for possible contingencies. This paper will address deliberate plans that primarily concentrate on situations when general deterrence and the TCP shaping operations have failed and a contingency situation exists in which leadership will employ military forces to achieve national objectives. The plans identify probable scenarios and develop synchronized courses of action in which military forces will execute operations to support national policy. Each plan has six phases beginning with Phase 0 and terminating at the end of Phase 5.

Phase 0, Shape, includes additional shaping activities specific to the deliberate plan. During this phase, the plan focuses on gaining access to the region through established basing rights and conducting combined training exercises with other nations in preparation for follow-on decisive operations. While Phase 1, Deter, is designed to deter hostilities, it primarily focuses on setting the environment for decisive and follow-on operations with some emphasis placed on an early understanding of the adversary decision maker.[22] During Phase 2, Seize the Initiative, and Phase 3, Dominate, military operations focus on applying combat power to immobilize enemy aggression and defeat the enemy's will to fight. In Phase 4, Stabilize, joint forces might perform governance functions in preparation for transitioning operations to civil authorities during Phase 5, Enable Civil Authority.

Concept and operation plans focus on the military response to a proposed enemy course of action that the United States seeks to deter. Until the trigger event happens

---

[22] U.S. Joint Chiefs of Staff, *Joint Publication 3-0*, V-4.

indicating deterrence has failed, specific actions to influence adversary decision makers are limited. Planners place some emphasis on understanding the adversary decision maker's cost benefit calculus but most intelligence analysis requests focus on enemy centers of gravity and military capabilities. Then the plans primarily use the punishment deterrence method in phases 2 and 3 to influence the decision maker's cost benefit calculus and defeat the enemy's will.

Combatant command level strategies are narrower in scope than national and departmental level strategies. The TCP documents a general deterrence strategy directed towards influencing regional audiences while the concept and operation plans provide an immediate deterrence strategy directed toward a specific state or non-state actor. However, planners have a limited understanding of the specific adversary decision maker's cost benefit calculus. Since these strategies do not identify specific decision makers to influence, developing measures of effectiveness before deterrence fails is difficult. Additionally, mechanisms to integrate and synchronize deterrence operations across all elements of national power require improvement.

With the exception of concept and operation plans, the U.S. has continued to develop general deterrence strategies. While these strategies have evolved from having only a military force focus to implementing all instruments of national power, integrating and synchronizing deterrence activities and messages across departments is problematic. Establishing an organization to integrate and synchronize deterrence operations across all departments would provide unity of effort for deterrence operations.

U.S. deterrence strategies do not incorporate the limited guidance contained in the DO JOC. Specifically, the strategies do not identify the leaders, decision makers or influencers the United States wants to deter nor do they identify specific actions the adversary should or should not take. Instead, the strategies focus on global and regional audiences and do not focus on influencing specific decision makers. Since deterrence operations are designed to influence a decision maker's cost benefit calculus, it is difficult to measure the effectiveness deterrence operations have on unknown decision makers.

A detailed joint deterrence doctrine would assist planners in developing better deterrence strategies. Until one is written, planners need to better incorporate the few fundamental principles when developing deterrence strategy. The next chapter will examine historical cases and deterrence activities to gain insight into possible indicators that planners can use to measure the effectiveness of deterrence activities. Furthermore, a similar doctrine, Military Deception Doctrine, will be examined in Chapter 4 for fundamental principles that planners can use to successfully deter adversary decision makers.

CHAPTER 3
HISTORICAL CASES

The United States has continually engaged in deterrence activities and has sent deterrence messages achieving mixed results. This chapter will examine four historical diplomatic and military deterrence activities and analyze the resulting success or failures. The examination will begin with events and activities aimed at influencing Japan before the attack on Pearl Harbor and U.S. deterrence activities to end World War II. Next, a study of U.S. and the Union of Soviet Socialist Republics (U.S.S.R.) general deterrence activities that escalated to the Cuban Missile Crisis will be examined. A study of U.S. and Libyan relations from 1981 to 2003 will highlight how employing all instruments of national power and changing strategy can eventually prove successful. The final historical case reviews the events and activities used to influence Iraqi leaders prior to Gulf War I. After reviewing the four historical cases, this chapter will discuss military activities that support deterrence messages and provide considerations for future operations.

Japan 1941 - 1945

In order to dissuade Japan's further aggression against Asian countries, the United States declared an oil and steel trade embargo against Japan in July 1941. Additionally, the United States demanded Japan surrender all of its territorial gains since 1931 and return control to China and French Indo-China as a condition to lift the embargo. These actions did not deter Japan from continued aggression. In fact, due to Japan's dependence on U.S. trade for economic prosperity, Japan felt threatened by the U.S. coercive policy. The Japanese calculated that if they did not take action now, the embargo would strangle their economic prosperity and naval strength within two years and despite the costs of a war with the United States, the absence of action was worse than taking immediate action with high risks.[1] Therefore, U.S. diplomatic and economic deterrence options created a threat that provoked Japan's aggression against the United States vice deterring aggression.

In August 1941, Assistant Secretary of State Dean Acheson stated "no rational Japanese could believe an attack on us could result in anything but disaster for his country."[2] However, Japanese leaders believed that they could win if the conflict with the United States was limited and of short duration. They calculated that the attack on Pearl Harbor would cripple U.S. forces in the Western Pacific, break the will of the American people and facilitate negotiations.[3] What the Japanese failed to consider was how the surprise attack on Pearl Harbor would mobilize American citizens into action to fight and support a total war no matter the duration.

Despite an abundance of indicators, the Japanese attack on Pearl Harbor found the U.S. military ill prepared and the attack surprised U.S. leadership and the public. Japan's attempts to mask movements of military forces combined with poor coordination and information sharing between political and military personnel led U.S. military leaders to disregard the warning signs. In the months prior to the attack, the many diplomatic communiqués indicated Japan would attack. In fact, Japanese Ambassador Joseph C. Grew warned of "an all-out, do-or-die attempt, actually risking national hara-kiri...a suicidal struggle with the United States. While national sanity dictates against such

---

[1] Richard Betts, *Surprise Attack: Lessons for Defense Planning* (Washington DC: The Brookings Institution, 1982), 133-138.
[2] Keith Payne, *The Fallacies of Cold War Deterrence and a New Direction* (Lexington: The University Press of Kentucky, 2001), 1.
[3] Geoffrey Parker, ed., *Cambridge Illustrated History of Warfare: The Triumph of the West* (New York: Cambridge University Press, 2000), 333.

action, Japanese sanity cannot be measured by American standards of logic."[4] However, U.S. leadership disregarded Grew's warning due to their belief that Japan would not risk opening up another front. Japan's continued negotiation attempts to lift the trade embargo also influenced U.S. leadership to disregard Grew's warnings.

The United States, China and the United Kingdom confirmed their support for future military efforts against Japan in the December 1943 Cairo Declaration. This action further emboldened Japanese resolve. The Allies stated that military operations would continue until Allied forces gained control of all territories that Japan had seized since 1914 and Japan returned the territories of Manchuria, Formosa and Pescadores to the Republic of China. Finally, the declaration demanded an unconditional surrender of Japan.[5] Of the three requirements levied against Japan, Japanese leaders considered the return of the Chinese territories and the unconditional surrender unacceptable. Instead of creating a fear of consequences, the declaration increased Japanese resolve to continue fighting.

The United States attempted to deter further Japanese aggression using diplomacy through the 1945 Potsdam Proclamation stating "the full application of military power, backed by our resolve, *will* mean the inevitable and complete destruction of the Japanese armed forces and just as inevitably the utter devastation of the Japanese homeland."[6] While the Japanese Imperial leadership received and analyzed the Potsdam Proclamation, they discounted the credibility of the terms. They did not believe the United States had the will of the people to continue the war due to the heavy casualties the United States would incur by invading mainland Japan.

---

[4] Betts, 136.
[5] Robert Butow, *Japan's Decision to Surrender* (Stanford: Stanford University Press, 1954), 241.
[6] Ibid., 243.

Not until August of 1945 did U.S. attempts at deterrence succeed. The United States

detonation of the atomic bomb on Hiroshima and Nagasaki, Japan demonstrated its

capability to impose unacceptable costs. The 78,150 casualties in Hiroshima and the

37,000 casualties in Nagasaki,[7] along with the physical devastation, created a fear of

consequence and influenced Japanese leadership's belief that further aggression could

result in the extinction of Japan. This Emperor articulated this belief in his public address

on 14 August 1945:

> The enemy has begun to employ a new and most cruel bomb, the power of which to do damage is indeed incalculable, taking the toll of many innocent lives. Should We continue to fight, it would not only result in an ultimate collapse and obliteration of the Japanese nation, but also it would lead to the total extinction of human civilization. Such being the case, how are We to save the millions of Our subjects; or to atone Ourselves before the hallowed spirits of Our Imperial Ancestors? This is the reason why We have ordered the acceptance of the provisions of the Joint Declaration of the Powers.[8]

Throughout the war, U.S. leadership failed to understand the economic importance of

Japanese expansion and the desperateness the embargos created and the impacts the

territorial return and unconditional surrender demands had on the Japanese Imperial

culture. Failing to consider how the Japanese actually perceived the U.S. embargo and

poor information sharing between departments, blinded leaders to the possibility of an

attack. Failing to understand the Japanese Imperial culture and the demand for

unconditional surrender prolonged the war instead of bringing the war to an earlier end.

U.S. leaders must overcome misunderstandings of enemy thought processes and the

belief that no nation would attack due to America's strong military strength and power.

---

[7] The Home Office and the Air Ministry, *The Effects of the Atomic Bombs at Hiroshima and Nagasaki: Report of the British Mission to Japan* (London: His Majesty's Stationery Office , 1946), 18.
[8] Butow, 248.

Cuban Missile Crisis

The Cuban missile crisis provides an example of where general deterrence actions failed and the resulting immediate deterrence actions succeeded. The subsequent result was a general deterrence strategy that became successful again.[9]

In the late 1950s to early 1960s, leaders in the Soviet Union feared an imbalance of power between the United States and the Soviet Union. The overinflated claims in the numbers and capabilities of Intercontinental Ballistic Missiles Nikita Khrushchev made created the "missile gap" and played upon the fears of the American public. As a result, the United States placed Jupiter missiles in Turkey in response to Soviet threats and claims of superiority. Additionally, in late 1961 the United States invalidated the Soviet's claim to strategic superiority. This further exacerbated Khrushchev's and other Soviet leaders' fear and motivated them to place missiles in the Western Hemisphere to inflict the same kind of fear on Americans.

In August 1962, U.S. intelligence personnel documented the positioning of Soviet surface-to-air missiles in Cuba and concluded that the Soviets would not introduce strategic missiles or create a Soviet military base in Cuba. Additionally, U.S. leadership held the same belief as National Security Advisor McGeorge Bundy who believed that the Soviets would not "do anything as crazy from our standpoint as placement of Soviet nuclear weapons in Cuba" which would risk nuclear war. [10] Therefore, in September 1962, President Kennedy issued two public statements warning the Soviet Union that the United States would consider it unacceptable for the Soviet Union to place offensive missiles in Cuba and that the United States would use "whatever means may be

---

[9] Lebow and Stein, *When Does Deterrence Succeed*, 16.
[10] Payne, 11-12.

necessary" to prevent Cuba from conducting offensive actions against countries in the

Western Hemisphere. [11] Additionally, with Cuba becoming an issue in the November

congressional elections and to calm the American public, President Kennedy's statements

confirmed that the Soviets had shipped defensive missiles and other military equipment

to Cuba but emphasized no evidence of offensive weapons build-up existed. Soviet

Union leadership viewed the warnings as political statements directed towards the

American public vice threats directed at the Soviet Union; therefore, they continued the

movement of medium range offensive missiles to Cuba.

Upon discovering the arrival of strategic missiles in Cuba in October 1962, Kennedy

faced a dilemma; do nothing and allow the Soviet Union to deploy offensive missiles in

Cuba or show resolve and risk escalating to nuclear war. Kennedy believed Khrushchev

to be rational and that when confronted Khrushchev would alter his position; therefore,

Kennedy chose to show America's resolve. To control escalation, Kennedy decided to

impose a limited naval blockade and threaten air strikes to destroy the missiles if the

Soviet Union did not remove them. Khrushchev agreed to withdraw the missiles from

Cuba after the United States effectively imposed an embargo, threatened to conduct air

strikes and secretly agreed to withdraw the Jupiter missiles from Turkey.

Khrushchev miscalculated Kennedy's resolve and considered the strategic threat from

the United States high enough to accept the risk associated with deploying missiles to

Cuba. Khrushchev also believed he could manage any associated risk arising from

deploying the missile and avoid the confrontation from escalating to total war.

---

[11] John F. Kennedy Library, *White House Diary, September 5, 1962.*
http://whd.jfklibrary.org/Diary/NYT/New%20York%20Times%20Chronology%20September%201962.ht
m (accessed March 14, 2010).

Furthermore, Khrushchev also used this as a bargaining tool similar to the 1961 Berlin crisis to show Soviet resolve to counter balance U.S. power.

The United States must communicate unambiguous and credible deterrence messages. Khrushchev did not consider Kennedy's September messages as credible since he perceived that Kennedy aimed the messages toward the American public and not the Soviet Union. Contributing to this belief, Khrushchev viewed the American people as timid towards nuclear war, weak and irresolute. He also calculated that Kennedy's youthfulness equated to inexperience; therefore, the messages did not create a credible threat.

Misperceptions by both leaders led to deterrence actions and messages that did not deter but provoked a response due to a perceived imbalance of power between the nations. Krushchev's propaganda about their strategic missile capabilities contributed to an arms race and caused the United States to deploy the Jupiter missiles to Turkey. The Soviet Union viewed this deterrence action as an unacceptable threat and in turn deployed their missiles to Cuba. The secret negotiations to remove the Jupiter missiles allowed Kennedy to avoid military escalation and avoid potential political consequences. At the same time Khrushchev perceived he had no choice but to remove the missiles from Cuba or have them destroyed by the United States. Using the security of its military superior strategic weapons to deter along with diplomatic negotiations, the United States compelled the Soviet Union to remove the missiles from Cuba thus deterring an attack.

Libya 1981 - 2003

U.S. deterrence activities and messages targeting Libyan leader Muammar Qaddafi eventually proved successful in achieving U.S. objectives to deter Libyan support to terrorist organizations and countering weapons of mass destruction (WMD) development. Relations with Qaddafi began deteriorating in the 1970s due to his illegal claims on international waters and his support to terrorist organizations. Not until the Reagan Administration did the United States begin actively confronting Qaddafi's illegal activities.

With the objective of regime change, the Reagan Administration began challenging Qaddafi's claim that Libyan territory included the Gulf of Sidra which violated international waters conventions. The U.S. military began naval show of force exercises in the Gulf of Sidra in 1981. Until 1986, Libyan reactions included non-hostile military actions and increased rhetoric from Qaddafi staking his claim to the international waters. Tension between the United States and Libya increased after the Libyan seizure of the *Achille Lauro* and the Rome and Vienna airport bombings in 1985. In March 1986, U.S. military naval forces operating in the Gulf of Sidra drew hostile fire from the Libyan military. Embarrassed by the U.S. military's prevailing response to the Libyan aggression, Qaddafi ordered terrorist attacks resulting in the bombing of the La Belle discotheque in West Berlin which killed two U.S. soldiers and injured more than seventy Americans.[12]

The United States did not let the discotheque bombing go unanswered. In April 1986, the United States conducted air strikes against five Libyan targets. Planners selected the targets based upon the target's relationship to supporting terrorist activities and to protect U.S. aircraft from counter air strikes. In the aftermath, the international community condemned the attacks; however, many U.S. allies increased their support to countering

---

[12] Bruce Jentelson and Christopher Whytock, "Who 'Won' Libya? The Force-Diplomacy Debate and Its Implications for Theory and Policy," *International Security,* 30, no 3 (Winter 2005/06): 58.

terrorist activities. The attacks had a profound impact on Qaddafi. While he still supported terrorist activities, he did so quietly and not with the public rhetoric previously seen.

The Reagan Administration also employed diplomatic and economic instruments of national power in an effort to dissuade Qaddafi's continued support to terrorist organizations and prevent Libya from acquiring WMD technology. Between 1982 and 1985 the United States attempted to rally support from other nations to mirror the U.S. Embassy closing in Libya and garner support for trade embargos for oil products. Lacking support from other nations, the unilateral U.S. actions did not significantly impact the Libyan economy or decrease public support for Qaddafi.

The United States continued to gather intelligence on Libyan terrorist activities and WMD acquisition efforts but did not engage militarily with Libya after 1986. After the December 1988 bombing of Pan Am Flight 103 over Lockerbie, Scotland, the G.H.W. Bush Administration gained international support to U.S. initiatives against Libya. United Nations Resolutions in 1992 and 1993 demanded Libya disclose all information on Pan Am Flight 103, accept responsibility for the role Libyan leadership played, renounce terrorism and compensate the victim's families.[13]

The Clinton Administration secured United Nation sanctions prohibiting outside support to the Libyan aircraft industry and supplying parts and technology for Libyan oil and gas infrastructure which increased the pressure on Qaddafi.[14] These multilateral sanctions combined with the drop in oil prices significantly impacted the Libyan

---

[13] United Nations, *Security Council Resolutions - 1993: Resolution 883: Libyan Arab Jamahiriya,* 11 Nov 1993, http://daccess-dds-ny.un.org/doc/UNDOC/GEN/N93/626/78/PDF/N9362678.pdf?OpenElement (accessed March 9, 2011).
[14] Ibid.

economy in the 1990s. Eventually, the economic crisis evolved into public unrest and the rise of radical groups within Libya. As a result of the internal domestic pressures combined with international pressure and Qaddafi's desire to preserve his regime, his noncompliance with accepted international practices in the early 1990s gave way to countering terrorist groups such as Al Qaeda and complying with international demands later in the decade.

Desperate for American oil infrastructure parts and technology to invigorate the economy, Qaddafi began secret negotiations with the United States in 1992. Libya would stop its pursuit of WMD in response to lifting the sanctions. The United States insisted Libya resolve all United Nation requirements for the Pan Am incident before the United States would lift the sanctions. The United Nation lifted the international sanctions after Libya surrendered personnel connected with the Pan Am bombing. However, the United States continued to enforce the unilateral trade sanctions awaiting Libyan leadership to accept responsibility and compensate the victim's families.

The Clinton and G.W. Bush Administrations continued to increase international pressure on Qaddafi by publicly highlighting Libya's treaty violations, disclosing the construction of a chemical weapons facility and reporting the intercept of nuclear technology shipments. They continued to press Qaddafi to comply with the United Nations Resolutions from the Pan Am incident. Qaddafi slowly began to comply. He renounced terrorist activities in 1998 calling for the arrest of Osama bin Laden and he condemn the September 11, 2001 attacks on the United States. Libya accepted responsibility and agreed to compensate the victim's families in August 2003 resolving the Pan Am incident. Wanting to end international isolation, improve his international image and maintain his leadership position, Qaddafi officially announced abandoning Libya's nuclear and chemical weapons programs in December 2003.

Military deterrence activities and messages alone did not deter Libyan support to terrorist organizations or deter their pursuit of WMD. In fact, U.S. naval activity in the Gulf of Sidra provoked Qaddafi to order attacks against American targets, not deter them. Influencing Qaddafi to take the actions the United States desired required employing all U.S. instruments of national power and gaining support from the international community over a twelve year period. Eventually, Qaddafi renounced terrorist activities in 1998 and abandoned WMD programs in 2003.

Iraq 1990 - 1991

In the months prior to Iraq's invasion of Kuwait, U.S. leadership did not respond to Saddam Hussein's public statements and actions in time to deter his aggression. In February 1990, Saddam Hussein engaged in a series of public statements and discussions warning Arab nations to guard against the United States uncontested influence over the Arab Gulf region and its oil. He perceived that the Arab people would be "governed by the wishes of the United States."[15] Saddam continued his rhetoric in April when he remarked that his country had an effective chemical weapons capability and threatened to retaliate if Israel attacked Iraqi interests. Furthermore, Saddam began a series of accusations and threats targeted towards Kuwait and the United Arab Emirates (U.A.E.).

In May 1990, Saddam accused Kuwait and the U.A.E. of producing oil over the Organization of Petroleum Exporting Countries (OPEC) quotas. He considered the over production an act of war using economic means. The over production had lowered the

---

[15] Alex Hybel, *Power Over Rationality: The Bush Administration and the Gulf Crisis* (New York: State University of New York Press, 1993), 34.

per barrel price of oil which had a negative economic impact on Iraq as they recovered

from the war with Iran. In July, Saddam used the accusation as justification for war in

his statement, "The oil quota violators have stabbed Iraq with a poison dagger. Iraq will

not forget the saying that cutting necks is better than cutting means of living, Oh God

Almighty, be witness that we have warned them!"[16]

Saddam further accused Kuwait of stealing oil from the Rumaila oil field and

demanded the return of $2.4 billion of profits.[17] Saddam also demanded Kuwait forgive

the $40 billion debt Iraq accrued during the Iran-Iraq War.[18] He rationalized Iraq was

entitled to the relief since Iraq fought the war for all Arabs.

In addition to Saddam's public rhetoric, by mid July 1990, Iraqi forces had massed

along the Kuwait border. At this point, U.S. leaders believed it unlikely that one Arab

nation would attack another Arab nation and if an attack did occur, Iraq would conduct a

punitive and limited attack against Kuwait. Despite these beliefs, Secretary of Defense

Dick Cheney issued a warning to Saddam Hussein that the United States would "take

seriously any threats to U.S. interest or U.S. friends in the region."[19] To support this

statement, the United States prepared to deploy six warships to the Persian Gulf in a show

of force.

Many Arab leaders believed that Saddam used his own show of force capabilities to

coerce Kuwait into complying with his demands and they concluded that Iraq and Kuwait

could resolve the dispute peacefully. Also, as Iraq recovered from the eight years war

with Iran, others believed that Iraq would not risk a costly attack against Kuwait.

---

[16] John Stoessinger , *Why Nations Go To War* (Boston: Bedford/St. Martin's, 2001), 197.
[17] Micah Sifry and Christopher Cerf, eds., *The Gulf War Reader: History, Documents, Opinions* (New York: Time Books, 1991), 64.
[18] Stoessinger, 196.
[19] Hybel, 37.

However, the U.A.E. took Saddam's threats seriously and requested the United States show their military support through a joint exercise. The United States conducted a joint refueling exercise with the U.A.E. but other Arab leaders warned the United States not to provoke Saddam through U.S. military rhetoric.

To reinforce the military show of force actions, the United States Ambassador April Glaspie met with Saddam Hussein on July 25, 1990. Glaspie emphasized the Bush Administration's desire to improve relations between the United States and Iraq. She inquired about Iraq's intentions with regard to the massing of troops on the Kuwait border and reported Saddam had no intentions of taking action against Kuwait unless the countries could not resolve the dispute through negotiations. Saddam, in turn, inquired whether the Bush Administration would support Iraq or Kuwait and how would Washington respond to an invasion of Kuwait? Glaspie responded, "We have no opinion on the Arab-Arab conflicts, like your border disagreement with Kuwait."[20] Eight days after the meeting, Iraqi troops invaded Kuwait much to the surprise of the world.

The United Nations Security Council immediately condemned Iraq's invasion of Kuwait, demanded that Iraq withdraw immediately and called for Iraq and Kuwait to begin negotiations. Over the next five months, the United States imposed economic trade sanctions, built coalition support for the defense of Saudi Arabia and liberating Kuwait and began flowing forces into the region. At the same time, the United Nations passed a series of resolutions culminating in a January 15, 1991 deadline for Iraq to withdraw

---

[20] Sifry and Cerf, 115.

from Kuwait and authorized the use of any means for member states to implement the resolutions.[21]

On several occasions during the five months prior to January 15, 1991, Saddam Hussein voiced his belief that "Americans were too cowardly to fight"[22] and claimed he would be victorious in war. Also, in a conversation with Ambassador Glaspie, Saddam stated,

> If you use pressure, we will deploy pressure and force. We know that you can harm us, although we do not threaten you. But we too can harm you...You can come to Iraq with aircraft and missiles, but do not push us to the point where we cease to care. And when we feel that you want to injure our pride and take away the Iraqis' chance of a high standard of living, then we will cease to care, and death will be the choice for us. Then we would not care if you fired 100 missiles for each missile we fired. Because without pride life would have no value.[23]

Just before the deadline, President Bush attempted to encourage Iraqi forces to leave Kuwait in a letter to Saddam Hussein. The letter warned "Iraq cannot and will not be able to hold on to Kuwait or exact a price for leaving."[24] Furthermore, President Bush emphasized that Saddam should not underestimate the will of the American people to free the people of Kuwait and restore its government. Despite the efforts of the United States, Arab leaders and members of the United Nations, Iraqi forces did not leave Kuwait by the deadline.

Deterrence efforts did not succeed primarily because Saddam Hussein did not believe the United States would risk casualties by retaliating. Based upon his observation that

---

[21] United Nations. *Security Council Resolutions - 1991: Resolution 678: Iraq-Kuwait,* 29 Nov 1991, http://daccess-dds-ny.un.org/doc/RESOLUTION/GEN/NR0/575/28/IMG/NR057528.pdf?OpenElement (accessed March 9, 2011).
[22] Stoessinger, 203.
[23] Sifry and Cerf, 125-126.
[24] The American Presidency Project, *George Bush: Statement by Press Secretary Fitzwater on President Bush's Letter to President Saddam Huessin of Iraq, January 12, 1991.* http://www.presidency.ucsb.edu/ws/index.php?pid=19214&st=&st1=#axzz1OJnqVyOu (accessed September 6, 2010).

the United States only conducted an air war over Bosnia and the United States responded to terrorist attacks with stand-off missile strikes against terrorist training camps, Saddam concluded the United States wanted to avoid another Vietnam. Additionally, Saddam did not believe that the American public would support a war. Due to his perceptions, the United States could not create a credible threat or create a fear of consequence.

General Supporting Activities

Many activities in which the U.S. military participates support a strategy of deterrence through deterrent options. These deterrent options should also support Theater Campaign Plans, as well as, concept and operations plans. While planners focus the activity to influence audiences in one nation, leaders must realize many nations watch and interpret the intent behind U.S. military actions. The following paragraphs examine the effects some military deterrent options can create and highlight what planners should consider before executing them.

The United States has maneuvered carrier groups and flown demonstration flights off the coast of countries to show resolve supporting diplomatic relations. While force projection activities can peacefully resolve conflicts as in the coup attempt against President Aquino, they can also provoke a response as demonstrated in Libya.

Naval vessel port visits and basing rights for air and land forces enhance diplomatic ties and show commitment to extended deterrence operations. The forward presence of U.S. forces demonstrates the ability to respond rapidly during crisis situations and provides a deterrence effect. Inactivity within a theatre of operation or country can have a negative deterrence effect. Chinese military leaders noted this when they viewed U.S. support to Taiwan with skepticism. "U.S. military forces have not, they noted, conducted military exercises with Taiwan for two decades and U.S. warships no longer visit the island to demonstrate support."[25]

Joint and combined exercises demonstrate maneuverability, interoperability and destructive capabilities. Additionally, these exercises strengthen alliances. Most readiness exercise objectives look internally to assess capabilities like the command and control of forces, integrating new capabilities, and logistic movements, but the exercise does not target specific adversary decision makers. Sometimes combined exercises can heighten tensions within a region. Shortly after North Korea bombed a South Korean island in November 2010, the U.S. and South Korea continued preparations for an already scheduled naval exercise. The exercise provoked North Korea to warn that the combined exercises could provoke an all out war. Exercise objectives should include what an adversary decision maker should conclude from observing the exercise. This will drive an assessment of what regional states or adversaries observed the exercise and potentially how the observers perceived the exercise and their reaction.

Operational tests and evaluations of weapon systems such as intercontinental ballistic missiles or missile defense interceptors display the accuracy and destructive capabilities of weapons. New capabilities can create a perceived vulnerability in the adversary's capabilities as evidenced by Russia's claims that U.S. missile defense radars in Poland would threaten the defense capabilities and security of Russia.

Planners design military deterrent options to de-escalate the crisis situation to allow an early resolution acceptable to both parties. However, as evidenced in the previous paragraphs, the adversary may view these options as a provocation that requires a

---

[25] Payne, 156.

response. Leadership must consider the adversary decision makers possible responses and weigh the risks before executing deterrent options.

The four historical cases and the military deterrent options demonstrate the United States conducts military operations without fully understanding the beliefs and perceptions of the adversary decision maker. Additionally, before executing operations, planners must consider how the adversary will respond to deterrence activities. Without fully understanding the adversary decision maker's beliefs and possible reactions, measuring deterrence effectiveness proved ineffective. Finally, these examples highlight the importance of integrating and synchronizing activities using all instruments of national power to achieve deterrence objectives. Chapter 4 will examine military deception doctrine to understand how to plan operations that influence an adversary decision maker into taking the desired action.

CHAPTER 4
MILITARY DECEPTION OPERATIONS

Similar to deterrence operations, military deception operations also influence the actions of an adversary decision maker. This chapter will discuss the basics of the military deception planning process followed by a look at three historical deception executions and their outcomes. The first is the highly successful Operation MINCEMEAT where deception planners used a dead body with planted documents to convince the German High Command that the allies would invade southern Europe at Sardinia and Greece. The second deception plan, Operation CAMILLIA, successfully relayed its message but did not successfully achieve the desired enemy action at the battle at Abyssinia. The final deception plan, Operation STARKEY, completely failed due to the fact that the adversary decision maker viewed the deception story as implausible. This chapter will conclude with military deception operations lessons learned that planners can apply to deterrence operations and develop alternative measures of effectiveness.

Military Deception Planning

Military forces conduct deceptive operations to cause an enemy to take an action or inaction in which the outcome is favorable to friendly successful mission accomplishment. Deception plans do not stand alone but support a Combatant Commanders' Operations Plans. Since the deception operation only supports an existing operations plan, planners need to ensure the overall military operation will succeed even if the deception plan does not cause the desired enemy action. Clearly stated deception goals determine how the deception plan contributes to successful mission accomplishment. Clearly defined deception objectives state what action the adversary will or will not take as a result of deceptive operations.

In addition to the military principles of war, Joint Publication 3-13.4 identifies six military deception principles that provide guidance in planning and executing deceptive operations.[1] The first principle properly focuses deception activities by identifying the adversary decision maker or organization that can take or direct the desired adversary action or inaction. Once identified, planners must understand the dynamics associated with how the decision maker(s) obtains and analyzes information, what they are predisposed to believe, and what motivates them to action. During this process, planners must objectively analyze how the adversary thinks to avoid introducing mirror-imaging prejudices.

The second principle recommends clearly defined military deception objectives to focus friendly actions and resources to cause the adversary to take a specific action.[2] Similar to unity of command, centralized planning and control is the third military deception principle. This ensures planners synchronize military deception operations with real world operations to avoid conflicts in achieving mission success. Strict compliance in applying need-to-know criteria supports the fourth principle of security. Planners accomplish this by minimizing the number of personnel witting to the military deception plan. Only a few personnel will have full disclosure of the military deception operation, while most supporting operations personnel will have limited knowledge consistent with their particular portion of the operation. The last two principles are timeliness and integration. Developing, planning and executing deceptive operations

---

[1] U.S. Joint Chiefs of Staff, *Joint Publication 3-13.4: Military Deception* (Washington DC: Government Printing Office, July 2006), I-5.
[2] Ibid.

requires an appropriate amount of lead time to allow the adversary time to detect, analyze and react before the actual mission execution. Due to the significant lead time required, deception planning should start at the beginning of concept of operations development for the parent plan. This will ensure full integration of the deceptive operations during mission execution.

Planners must make military deception operations believable through words, actions and capabilities. They accomplished this by targeting the adversary decision maker's information collection conduits to communicate the deception story. The adversary decision maker must observe deception activities, develop conclusions as to friendly force intentions and then act. Planners employ a variety of physical, technical and administrative means to convey the deceptive story. During deception operations execution, planners seek operational and analytical feedback to assess the effectiveness of deceptive activities.

Operational feedback determines what deceptive information reached the desired decision maker and analytical feedback determines what actions or inactions the decision maker takes based upon the received information. Planners develop measures of effectiveness using quantifiable indicators to assess how well the deception plan achieved its goals. Did the adversary take the desired action or inaction? What the planner will not know is why the adversary did or did not take the desired action or inaction. Planners generally do not receive this type of direct feedback during execution and may not obtain direct feedback until many months or years after operations have ended, if at all.

Deception Operations

Operation MINCEMEAT: Planning for Operation MINCEMEAT began almost one year prior to executing Operation HUSKY, the allied invasion of Sicily. Deception planners designed MINCEMEAT to convince the German High Command that allied forces would invade Sardinia and Greece with the goal of protecting the allied force invasion site of Sicily. Planners developed deception activities around the objective of preventing or delaying German counter forces from massing in Sicily.

MINCEMEAT targeted the decision maker, Adolph Hitler, using intelligence conduits in Spain. The deception reinforced Hitler's fear of an attack through the Balkans and at the same time discredited Sicily as the location since it was too obvious a choice. Deception planners also knew an active German agent with strong connections to Spaniard officials operated in Huelva, Spain. By targeting the Spanish operatives, planners took advantage of the fact that the German intelligence network in Spain quickly processed information without conducting a detailed validation before forwarding the information to higher authorities.

To feed information to Hitler and make the plan plausible, planners developed the full identity of a fictional Major Martin, Royal Marines to include personal documents and job expertise. Additionally, Major Martin would transport high level personal letters between generals at Combined Operations Headquarter and generals in the Mediterranean on his flight to North Africa. The deceptive personal letters indicated allied forces would land in Sardinia and Greece and not Sicily since Sicily was too obvious. Planners carefully prepared a dead body, which would appear to have drowned as a result of the plane crash, and gave it Major Martin's identity. Based upon water currents, planners carefully selected a location in the Mediterranean Sea to release the body and planted papers in hopes that the body would float to the coast near Huelva, Spain.

Planners received operational feedback that the body had reached Huelva through official notifications from the Spanish Consulate. Additionally, Spanish officials returned the black brief case containing the personal letters to the Madrid Naval Attaché ten days later. Indirect operational feedback came from analyzing the envelopes which revealed someone had removed two of three letters from their sealed envelopes. Planners concluded Hitler's information conduits received the deceptive information.

Planners received indirect analytical feedback via the relatively unopposed allied invasion of southern Sicily. They did not receive direct feedback until one year later through captured documents seized at Tambach which confirmed the German High Command's belief that allied forces would invade Sardinia and Greece.[3] As a result, German forces maneuvered to defend Greece and they increased fortifications of Sardinia and Corsica. German forces did not readjust to the allied invasion of Sicily until two days after Operation HUSKY started.

Operation MINCEMEAT's clearly defined goals and objectives, the planner's patience and understanding of information conduits to reach the decision maker and full integration into Operation HUSKY ensured success. Operation CAMILLA did not have the same level of success. While Operation CAMILLA did successfully influence the decision maker, the planners focused on what the adversary must think and not on what the planners wanted the adversary to do.

Operation CAMILLA: "A" Force, which consisted of Dudley Clarke and one other officer at the time, developed their first deception plan codenamed Operation CAMILLA.

---

[3] Ewen Montagu, *The Man Who Never Was* (Philadelphia: J.B. Lippincott Company, 1954), 126.

Planners wanted the Italian forces to believe that allied forces in Africa would attack Italian forces in Abyssinia (Ethiopia) from the south through Kenya and protect the real attack from British Somalia in the North. The desired objective intended for Italian forces to withdraw from the north and reinforce forces in the south.

Using radio deception, dummy equipment and false equipment and troop movements, the deception operation overwhelmingly convinced the Italians to believe that the allied attack from the south would succeed. The Italians withdrew their forces from the south, shortened their lines of communications and moved some of their forces to the north. The planners did not receive operational or analytical feedback until allied forces attacked and met a well defended northern flank at Keren and conducted unopposed operations in the south.

The overall campaign succeeded in defeating the Italian forces in Abyssinia but the deception did not enhance operations.[4] Planners learned that they must concentrate on what action they want the enemy to take in addition to what the enemy must think.

Operation STARKEY: Planners began developing Operation STARKEY only seven months prior to a fictitious September 1943 invasion. They wanted to convince the German High Command that allied forces planned to invade northwest France soon. The objective intended to occupy German forces in the Pas de Calais area and stop German forces in France from moving to reinforce German troops in Italy. The deception combined fictitious forces and dummy equipment in England with actual training raids in the Pas de Calais area to make the Germans believe a cross channel invasion was imminent. News and radio media overtly advertised the invasion window of September 1943.

---

[4] Jon Latimer, *Deception in War* (Woodstock: The Overlook Press, 2001), 61.

Operational feedback came when the cross channel training raids did not stimulate German intelligence interest. Analytical feedback came when a small force conducted unopposed invasion operations at Pas de Calais. The Germans believed the allies did not have sufficient forces to conduct a cross channel invasion. Additionally, they disregarded the abundance of information as to the planned invasion date since opposing forces would not readily advertise such a date. As a result of the ineffective deception, the Germans did not believe an invasion would occur and moved two-thirds of their forces from France to reinforce operations in Italy.[5]

Military Deception Operations Lessons Learned

Focus: The three deception operations emphasized the importance for planners to determine the focus of the deception plan. Operations MINCEMEAT and STARKEY targeted Hitler and the German High Command and Operation CAMILLA targeted the Italian forces in Abyssinia. The plans used various combinations of verbal, written and visual communication channels to relay the deception story. Only planners of Operation MINCEMEAT correctly understood the predisposition of the decision maker. They reinforced Hitler's fear of an attack through the Balkans by indicating landing sites in Greece. Planners also discredited the actual landing sites in Sicily as too obvious a choice; therefore, they indicated additional landing sites in Sardinia. From Operation STARKEY, planners learned it is harder to change the decision maker's perceptions and beliefs than to reinforce them. Hitler did not believe that allied forces would conduct a cross channel invasion immediately; therefore, he ignored the deception activities and maneuvered German forces from France to Italy.

---

[5] David Mure, *Master of Deception: Tangled Webs in London and the Middle East* (London: William Kimber and Company Limited, 1980), 225.

Objective: From Operation CAMILLA, planners learned the importance of clearly defining the objective; what is the desired enemy action or inaction? Planners successfully influenced what they wanted the adversary decision maker to think, but planners did not focus on what they wanted the adversary to do. If the fear of consequence is too great, the enemy may react in a way unfavorable to friendly forces. In the case of Operation CAMILLA, the Italians withdrew their forces from the south and reinforced their northern flank, the location of the actual allied attack.

Timeliness and Integration: Military deception operations require a long lead time to plan and execute. Planners require time to properly develop, integrate and execute the deception plan so that the adversary decision maker has time to detect and analyze the information and then react. Planning for Operation MINCEMEAT began in the summer of 1942 and the adversary's intelligence network detected the body on April 30, 1943. By May 14, 1943, Hitler believed the deception and maneuvered reinforcements to Greece and fortified Sardinia and Corsica. Hitler continued to believe the deception until two days after the allied invasion of Sicily began in July 1943.[6]

Credible: Planners must develop credible deception stories in order for the enemy to believe it. In Operation CAMILLA, the use of radio deception, dummy equipment and false equipment and troop movements created a credible threat, such that the Italians believed that the allies planned an overwhelming attack from the south. However, in Operation STARKEY, fictitious forces, dummy equipment and training raids did not create a credible threat. Therefore, Hitler did not believe the allies would conduct a cross channel invasion immediately.

---

[6] Montagu, 104-148.

Feedback: Operational and analytical feedback provide indicators that the deception plan may or may not work. Planners may not know how effective or ineffective the deception plan influenced the adversary decision maker until years after execution. During Operation MINCEMEAT, planners received operational and some analytical feedback immediately. Over one year after execution, planners received analytical feedback validating the huge success of the deception operation. Operation STARKEY's operational feedback indicated the adversary information conduits did not detect the activities and analytical feedback confirmed the ineffectiveness of the deception operation.

Support: Military operation plans must succeed even if the military deception plan does not. Planners properly resourced the main military operations for all three plans to succeed even if the deception failed. Operation CAMILLA clearly demonstrated this requirement when the deception activities actually degraded friendly operations by influencing the Italians to reinforce the northern flank.

Application to Deterrence Operations

Deterrence operations planners can apply the lessons learned from deception operations to create measureable deterrence plans. To successfully deter an adversary into taking an action or inaction favorable to friendly forces, deterrence plans must first have the proper focus. Planners must identify the specific adversary decision maker or organization that can take or direct the desired action. Once identified, planners must understand the adversary's predisposition and how they obtain information.

Planners should reinforce a decision maker's beliefs rather than change the decision maker's mind; therefore, deterrence activities should start early before the decision maker has committed to an unfavorable course of action. Identifying what specific action planners want the decision maker to take provides a clearly defined objective.

Deterrence operations require centralized planning and control and a long lead time to integrate, execute and measure. Therefore, the National Security Council should establish an organization to oversee all U.S. Government deterrence activities. This organization can use a matrix similar to the example at Table 1 to assist in synchronizing and integrating deterrence activities. This will ensure unity of deterrence efforts across all U.S. Government departments. A capable military force conducting flexible deterrence options support credible deterrence messages. However, military leaders and planners must develop sufficient force capability able to succeed should deterrence fail.

Once executed, planners should monitor for operational and analytical feedback to deterrence activities. Operational feedback confirms the adversary decision maker or information conduits observed and received the deterrence activity or message. Analytical feedback monitors for adversary actions or inactions as a result of the deterrence operation. Many times planners do not receive positive direct feedback until after the operation has terminated; therefore, absence of feedback should not stop future deterrence activities. Deterrence activities executed over a long period of time also allows planners to detect and analyze feedback information, adjust deterrence activities so that the adversary eventually takes the desired action.

Finally, military doctrine and planning guidance ensures lessons learned from previous operations are incorporated into future operations. Joint Staff should develop deterrence doctrine with a level of specificity similar to the detail contained in the military deception doctrine. The doctrine document should incorporate the requirement for developing focused deterrence plans with clearly defined objectives. It should emphasize the long lead time required to plan, integrate and execute deterrence activities. Finally, the deterrence doctrine should include recommendations for obtaining operational and analytical feedback and apply the data collected to measuring deterrence effectiveness.

EXAMPLE U.S. GOVERNMENT SYNCHRONIZATION MATRIX

DETERRENCE GOAL: Deter Country X, specifically President Jones, from supporting terrorist organizations

OBJECTIVE	WHEN/ DATE EXECUTED	ACTION	AGENCY	CONSIDERATIONS/FEEDBACK
				Common to all objectives: Did country X observe activity?
Counter weapons shipments	2 times in 20XX	Conduct interdiction combined exercise w/ neighboring nations	DoD	Did President Jones make public/private statements? How did Country X military respond?
Support neighboring nations and gain regional access	Monthly	Port visit, basing right surveys, military-to-military exchange	DoD	Did President Jones make public/private statements? Have political relations with country X changed? How did Country X military respond? Has Country X sought alliances with U.S. adversary nations?
Gain international support	Continual	Seek UN support to denounce Country X actions, impose trade embargo	DoS	Did President Jones respond to UN initiatives? Has Country X found alternative sources for trade embargo deficit? Has Country X economic prosperity changed?
Prevent financing support	Continual	Freeze financing assets. Obtain international support	DoT/DoS	Did President Jones make public/private statements about the impacts? Has Country X realigned internal financing?
Strategic communications	Continual	Public statements denouncing Country X/Pres Jones activities/Highlight U.S. intentions/resolve	USG	How did President Jones respond to U.S. statements? What support has Country X received from other nations? What response came from the international community? Are U.S. verbal comms consistent with physical activities?
Prevent sanctuary in surrounding nations	Continual	Promote governance FID	DoS/DoD	Has President Jones sought to influence surrounding nations? Has Country X military or terrorist support agencies moved to new locations? Do regional organizations support governance actions?

Table 1

CHAPTER 5
MEASURES OF EFFECTIVENESS

Deterrence strategy measures of effectiveness assist decision makers in determining if the deterrence strategy produced the desired effects. However, as discussed earlier, planners have a challenge to measure the effects of deterrence activities and messages since the adversary will not readily admit to being deterred. Planners can determine if the adversary does not take the undesired action but planners generally will not know why. Did the U.S. deterrence efforts work or did the adversary have another reason for not taking the undesired action? The adversary may have never intended to take the undesired action but gave the impression he would to influence negotiations. The adversary may have intended to take the undesired action but reconsidered for reasons not related to U.S. deterrence activities and messages, such as failure to obtain alliances, resource constraints or internal domestic issues.

To assist in developing alternative measures of effectiveness, this chapter will examine conclusions from four different studies of when and why deterrence succeeded or failed. Using the conclusions from the deterrence studies, this chapter will categorize the indicators leading up to the historical events studied in Chapter 3. These indicators provided evidence that U.S. deterrence activities and messages were failing. Finally, this chapter will propose a list of indicators that planners can use to obtain indirect feedback to measure the effectiveness of deterrence activities and messages.

Deterrence Theory Studies

Alexander George and Richard Smoke conducted the first comprehensive study of American foreign policy and deterrence after World War II. They focused their study on conventional deterrence theory and practice from the Berlin Blockade through the Cuban

Missile Crisis. George and Smoke concluded that deterrence strategy is an integral part

of American foreign policy and that political leaders should only employ its military

strength when negotiations and conciliation fail.[1] During negotiations, a nation must

demonstrate concern, commitment and motivation, and communicate its intentions.[2]

George and Smoke went on to propose that leaders should consider how deterrence

strategy will affect containment and the balance of power perceptions of the adversary.[3]

Finally, they recommended the use of positive incentives in addition to the developing a

fear of negative consequences.[4]

The study by Paul Huth and Bruce Russett tried to determine what makes immediate

extended deterrence work. They analyzed fifty-four cases of extended deterrence

between 1900 and 1980 and the interrelationship between general and immediate

deterrence. They concluded that effective immediate deterrence does not rely solely on

strategic military strength but also on ties between nation states.[5] Strong economic and

military ties between nations improved deterrence strategy success against another

nation's aggression. However, formal military alliances between two nations increase the

probability that an allied country will engage militarily if attacked therefore escalating the

chance of war.[6] Huth and Russett recommended maintaining and strengthening the ties

of mutual interest for deterrence to succeed in a global economy.[7]

---

[1] George and Smoke, *Deterrence in American Foreign Policy*, 590-599.

[2] Ibid., 52.

[3] Ibid., 602.

[4] Ibid., 590.

[5] Paul Huth and Bruce Russett, "What Makes Deterrence Work? Cases from 1900 to 1980," *World Politics* 36 (July 1984): 496-497.

[6] Ibid., 521.

[7] Ibid., 524.

A.F.K. Organski and Jacek Kugler studied why major wars begin by testing three models: balance of power, collective security and power transition."[8] They also examined the affect of nuclear weapons on deterrence. Organski and Kugler concluded that major wars begin when the aggressor's economic, social and political national powers overtake the dominant nation.[9] They determined that a nation's economic productivity and the government's ability to mobilize the human and material resources for a national cause have a greater influence on deterrence than its military capability.[10] Nations primarily use their national power to influence the behavior of another nation through persuasion, rewards and/or punishment. Organski and Kugler also noted that nations infrequently use military force to influence other nations due the high demands and costs involved in exercising this instrument of power.

Ned Lebow and Janice Stein analyzed all three case studies described above applying the case study conclusions to deterring rational and irrational actors. Lebow and Stein concluded that challengers motivated by need are harder to deter than challengers motivated by opportunity. Additionally, they discovered that once a challenger commits to aggressive action, deterrence efforts become less effective. Therefore, Lebow and Stein recommend deterrence activities and messages start before the challenger has committed to aggressive acts. Also, they concluded that diplomacy must reassure and reduce external pressure while increasing internal domestic pressure such that the challenger can perceive a diplomatic solution to achieving their goals.[11]

---

[8] A.F.K. Organski and Jacek Kugler, *The War Ledger* (Chicago: University of Chicago Press, 1980), 13.
[9] Ibid., 225.
[10] Ibid., 8, 208-209.
[11] Lebow and Stein, *When Does Deterrence Succeed*, 3, 69.

Lebow and Stein also developed four guiding principles for analyzing deterrence. The first principle is to analyze the defender's deterrence messages for credibility, clear communication and support by a capable military to inflict unacceptable cost. If the defender sends ambiguous or conflicting messages, the challenger perceives an uncommitted defender; therefore, the defender's deterrence messages lack credibility. Additionally, if the challenger does not believe the defender can inflict unacceptable costs then the deterrence messages become ineffective.[12]

The second principle to analyzing deterrence is to determine what motivates the adversary, opportunity, need, or a combination of the two. Adversaries motivated by opportunity usually do not take forceful actions when they perceive high risks and high costs would result from initiating aggressive actions. Lebow and Stein found that leaders motivated by political or domestic needs generally overestimate friendly force capabilities and underestimate the capabilities and resolve of the defending nation which impacts the leader's cost benefit analysis. Additionally, the more desperate the situation, as perceived by the aggressive leader, the more likely the defender's deterrence attempts will fail. In these desperate situations, the aggressor will take high risk actions at high costs since the aggressor perceives the risk of taking no action just as risky and costly. These high risk, high cost actions makes the aggressor appear irrational to the defender.[13]

The third principle is to analyze how the defender used reassurance to reduce fear and the perceived vulnerabilities of the adversary. Here the defender must clearly

---

[12] Ibid., 60-61.
[13] Ibid., 68.

communicate his intentions and interests to reduce the fear created by the perceived vulnerabilities. Failure to successfully alleviate the fears can escalate to war.[14]

The final principle used to analyze deterrence is the perceived context of the challenger and defender.[15] When the leaders of two nations perceive the other nation as the challenger, they both direct action to defend against the threat posed by the other nation. Both leaders perceive themselves as the defender and their resulting deterrence actions as legitimate. Continued deterrence actions by both nations create a security dilemma that can escalate to war. The Cuban Missile Crisis best demonstrates this complex issue. During the Cuban Missile Crisis, leaders from both the United States and the Soviet Union directed actions in response to what they perceived as a threat from the other nation. Both nations rationalized their actions as a legitimate defensive response. The Soviets felt threatened by the U.S. Jupiter missiles in Turkey and the United States felt threatened by Soviet missiles in Cuba.

Historical Indicators

Using the above case study conclusions and the lessons learned from the military deception operations in Chapter 4, the indications evident in the historical events contained in Chapter 3 can be grouped into six categories: political indications, alliances, economic considerations, understanding motivation, communication and military forces.

Political Indicators: Three political indicators can become apparent before the outbreak of crisis or war. The first indicator, declining political relations, occurred in all four situations. The United States relations with Japan began declining in 1931 when Japan started its expansion into China and then escalated to war when the United States

---

[14] Ibid., 70.
[15] Ibid., 73.

imposed the trade embargo. Prior to the Cuban Missile Crisis, relations between the United States and the U.S.S.R. began deteriorating with the 1948 Berlin Blockade and continued to decline throughout the Korean War and the 1961 Berlin Crisis. Skirmishes between the U.S. and Libyan militaries began occurring five years prior to the U.S. attacks on Libyan terrorist support facilities. Finally, relations between Iraq and its neighboring nations quickly deteriorated in the six months prior to Iraq's invasion of Kuwait. Despite this relatively short period, significant political strife indicators developed. The United States continued to engage politically for six more months before retaliating and coming to the aid of Kuwait.

The second political indicator is a change in leadership or internal domestic policy which can strain an already fragile relationship or improve relationships over time. In 1941, Japan's new government became politically aggressive under the leadership of General Tojo. Khrushchev came to power in 1953 and began challenging the United States politically in the late 1950s with his overinflated missile capabilities claims and the Berlin Blockade in 1961 escalating to the Cuban Missile Crisis in 1962. Qaddafi came to power after a successful military coup in 1969 and began challenging the international community in 1973 by declaring the Gulf of Sidra Libyan territory.[16] However, internal domestic pressure forced Qaddafi to change his policies by the late 1990s.

Increased public rhetoric by political leaders is the third political indicator. Public rhetoric contributes to declining political relations, as well as, reveals possible intentions. Khrushchev's exaggerated strategic missile capabilities claims highlighted his fear of strategic imbalance. The United States should have expected Soviet reciprocal actions to

---

[16] Brian Davis, *Qaddafi, Terrorism, and the Origins of the U.S. Attack on Libya* (New York: Praeger Publishers, 1990), 2.

balance the power. Muammar Qaddafi's territorial claims for international waters provoked U.S. challenges, which in turn, increased Qaddafi's anti-western rhetoric. After the 1986 attacks, Qaddafi's public statements decreased as his policy changed from one of supporting terrorism and pursuing WMD technology to one of renouncing terrorist activities and supporting counter proliferation activities. Saddam Hussein's public statements indicated disputes over oil production quotas and warned the violators that Iraq would take action if the violators did not meet their demands. Saddam's statements also indicated he had no fear of U.S. attacks and that the Iraqis would choose death to protect their pride and values.

Alliances: International support for economic sanctions and military operations strengthen deterrence strategies against adversary aggression. U.S. unilateral trade sanctions and military operations did little to influence the Libyan economy or deter Qaddafi's support to terrorism or his efforts to obtain weapons of mass destruction. After the United States gained international support for economic sanctions and increased counter terrorism efforts, then the deterrence strategy became effective.

Economic Considerations: Recognizing declining economic prosperity can assist planners in understanding the adversary's perceptions of the current situation. The U.S. steel and oil trade embargo significantly impacted Japan's economic prosperity since Japan's economy heavily relied upon U.S. trade. U.S. leadership did not fully appreciate the Japanese perception of the embargo and therefore did not adjust its policy towards Japan. In the case of Libya, a declining economy and internal unrest forced Qaddafi to resolve international differences in order to lift the multilateral trade embargos. Iraq's national debt and slow economic recovery after the Iran – Iraq War indicated the desperateness for increased oil revenues.

Understanding Motivation: Sun Tzu's statement, "know the enemy and know yourself,"[17] is as important today as it was in 500 BC. Strategic warning analyst Cynthia Grabo noted, "The perception of what the adversary is thinking and how important the current issue is to him is fundamental to our ability to understand what he will do."[18] As covered in Chapter 3, Dean Acheson could not understand how Japanese leaders could believe that Japan's attack on the United States would succeed the same as McGeorge Bundy could not understand how the Soviet Union could believe that the United States would tolerate the Soviet Union placing missiles in the Western Hemisphere. Both Acheson and Bundy failed to understand the adversary's thought process and motivation. This inhibited their ability to conceptualize what the adversary would do. Similarly, the demands for unconditional surrender and territorial returns underestimated Japanese Imperial resolve and delayed the Japanese surrender. Additionally, economic development needs and a desire to lessen U.S. influence in the region motivated Saddam's aggression and rhetoric.

Communication: The United States did not consistently and clearly communicate American resolve to take action against the Soviet Union's missile deployment and Iraq's aggression against Kuwait. In both instances, conflicting diplomatic and political messages lessened the credibility of military deterrence activities. Subsequently, Khrushchev and Saddam did not believe the United States would commit to a military engagement which gave them both freedom to continue their intended course of action.

[17] Sun Tzu, *The Art of War*, 84.
[18] Cynthia Grabo, *Anticipating Surprise: Analysis for Strategic Warning* (Washington, DC: Joint Military Intelligence College's Center for Strategic Intelligence Research, 2002), 86.

Furthermore, the United States did not effectively reassure Soviet leadership that placing the Jupiter missiles in Turkey supported U.S. treaty obligations in the defense of Europe. While the United States viewed this action as a defensive measure to counter possible Soviet aggression into Europe, the Soviet Union perceived these as offensive weapons which exacerbated the Soviet's perceived vulnerabilities to U.S. nuclear attacks. As a result, the Soviet Union began deploying missiles to Cuba which increased tensions between the two nations.

Military Forces: Military force maneuvers and equipment movement can indicate intent if properly interpreted and tracked. This is especially true when logistic support functions forward deploy in conjunction with the offensive forces. The combined movements can indicate preparations for offensive action and not just an exercise. U.S. intelligence analysts correctly noted Japan's naval force movements south, but lost their position prior to the Pearl Harbor attack. The inability to track Japan's naval force hindered U.S. analysts' ability to determine Japan's intent. However, analysts correctly determined the Soviet Union's intent to place missiles in Cuba after discovering strategic missile shipments bound for the Western Hemisphere.

Political and military leaders failed to properly interpret the intent behind Iraqi force movements along the Kuwait border. They considered the build-up as an Iraqi show of force to get Kuwait's concession to Iraq's demands rather than preparation for an actual invasion. Leaders, planners and analysts must consider the data as presented and not insert mirror-imaging prejudice to determine what the adversary intends to do.

Deterrence Measures of Effectiveness (MOE)

Deterrence MOEs analyze data to determine if the deterrence activities and messages, and deterrent options, are meeting the objectives and progressing towards the desired end state of deterring attacks against the United States and its allies. They answer, "Are we doing the right things?"[19] Planners should not confuse MOEs with measures of performance (MOP) and combat assessments which answer, "Are we doing things right?"[20] During the Vietnam War, U.S. leadership used MOPs to measure the effectiveness and progress against Vietcong initiatives. Leaders compared U.S. casualties with the number of Vietcong casualties to report progress in deterring communist aggression. This MOP did not consider the Vietcong's will to suffer extraordinary number of casualties to support their cause. As a result, U.S. leaders perceived that the U.S. military was winning the war since the Vietcong casualties significantly outpaced U.S. casualties. However, the casualty comparisons did not assess if U.S. military activities had the desired effect on the Vietcong's will to fight.

Measurements provide feedback as to an organization's capabilities, successes and shortfalls and can provide early warning signals only if the organization measures the right things and applies the outcomes appropriately. As Dean Spitzer noted, "most individuals and organizations don't get what they want because they don't measure what they really want!"[21] The Combatant Commander uses priority intelligence requirements (PIR) to focus intelligence information collection about the adversary. Planners develop

---

[19] U.S. Joint Chiefs of Staff, *Joint Publication 3-0,* IV-32.
[20] Ibid., IV-32. (JP 3-0)
[21] Dean Spitzer, *Transforming Performance Measurement: Rethinking the Way We Measure and Drive Organizational Success* (New York: AMACON Books, 2007), 14. Dean Spitzer is acknowledged as one of the worlds leading experts on performance measurements and management. He has assisted public and private organizations improve performance and has received recognition and awards for his accomplishments.

the PIRs for the commander and have a tendency to request information about the adversary's military force structure, capabilities and exercises along with troop movements. The information collected enables planners to correctly posture U.S. forces to defeat the adversary should deterrence fail. As a result, intelligence analysts report on the adversary's capabilities, morale of forces, critical links, key nodes, centers of gravity, high value targets and probable courses of action. Besides focusing on military capabilities, PIRs must focus on the adversary's reaction to all U.S. Government activities over a long period of time.

In addition to the PIRs, Combatant Commander's measure and collect friendly force data. However, the military tends to only focus on performance measurements for each deterrence activity and not the desired effect. Units report on the number of activities such as combined exercises, personnel trained, bombs dropped and the number of casualties vice analyzing if the tasks affected the adversary decision maker. Limited resources, as well as, the vagueness of U.S. deterrence strategy which does not target a specific adversary decision maker contribute to the problem of not measuring the effects. While determining if the military unit correctly accomplished the task is important, planners must measure the effects of those activities against the deterrence strategy objectives.

In addition to measuring the right things, organizations must turn the data into productive information. "Large organizations collect millions of data points every day, but few are able to establish the right environment for the effective use of that measurement."[22] Preceding crisis situations and war, volumes of information provide evidence that deterrence is failing, yet many times the adversary's actions surprise U.S.

---

[22] Ibid., 4.

leaders. Post analysis reveals that volumes of information the intelligence community collected buried the important key indicators. Additionally, various organizations collected the data, but the organizations did not properly share key information collected. To better determine the adversary's intent, leaders, planners and analysts must focus on the critical indicators that determine deterrence MOEs. Table 2 provides examples of critical indicators from each of the six categories previously highlighted.

Historically, U.S. leaders failed to understand the adversary decision maker's motivation and intent. As a result, leaders did not properly interpret the indicators presented; therefore, they failed to change U.S. deterrence strategies. These actions, in turn, created an unacceptable situation from the adversary decision maker's perspective and caused the adversary to escalate the conflict or conduct a surprise attack. Examples include Japan's attack on Pearl Harbor, the Soviet Union's missile deployments to Cuba and Iraq's invasion of Kuwait. Leaders tend to ignore the plethora of indicators since they fail to view them objectively. Instead, they use personal preconceptions of how the enemy will behave. As Douglas Pike, an expert on Vietnamese affairs, noted that Robert McNamara used flawed logic in analyzing what Ho Chi Minh would do because the Vietnamese "don't think like we do."[23]

As evident throughout this paper, planners cannot separate military deterrence activities and messages from diplomatic, information and economic activities. As Spitzer says, "measures must be aligned with strategy, and then integrated across the entire

---

[23] Lewis Sorley, *Thunderbolt: General Creighton Abrams and the Army of His Times* (New York: Simon and Schuster, 1992), 266.

organization."[24] To assess the effectiveness of deterrence activities, leaders, planners and analysts must consider indicators from all elements of national power, as well as, day-to-day shaping activities conducted as part of the Theater Campaign Plans. While no one indicator will create the entire picture of an adversary's thought process, in combination, over a period of time, the indicators can assist planners in determining the overall effectiveness of the deterrence strategy.

Determining the effects of friendly actions can challenge the analyst since the actions may only cause subtle changes in the adversary's behavior. However, deterrence activities and messages have a cumulative effect that analysts can measure if properly focused. Properly developed PIRs allow intelligence analysts to provide operational and analytical feedback for deterrence activities and messages. Planners should develop deterrence PIRs using specific objectives of who is being deterred and what action the decision maker should or should not take in response to key U.S. Government activities.

Questions that focus on deterrence indicators will vary depending upon the activity; however, one question is common to obtain operational feedback: Did the adversary decision maker's information conduit observe and/or receive the deterrence activity and/or message? Other questions associated with deterrence activities could include the following: Has the political relationship with the adversary decision maker changed? Has the adversary decision maker's public and private communication messages and themes changed? What economic impact has trade negotiations or embargos had? Has the adversary found alternative sources of supply for the deficit created by the U.S. trade embargo? What did the adversary's military and security forces do in response to U.S. Government actions?

---

[24] Spitzer, 53.

Political Indicators:		
	-	Declining political relations and negotiations
	-	Adversary support for radical movements that go against accepted international norms
	-	Restricted U.S. and allied activities within the nation
	-	Change of leadership in key positions
	-	Adversary decision maker public rhetoric
	-	Change in domestic policy
	-	Regime survival statements
	-	Communiqués content pressuring nations to take action or inaction
	-	Public statements containing anti-western sentiment
Alliances:		
	-	Changes in political, economic or military alliances
	-	Attempts to gain regional support for their cause
Economic Considerations:		
	-	Impact of trade embargos
	-	Gross domestic product change
	-	Economic growth rate change
	-	Employment rate impacts on internal public motivation and security
Motivation:		
	-	Adversary decision maker values
	-	Adversary cultural norms and accepted practices
	-	Key influencers to the decision maker
Communication:		
	-	Consistent political, military, economic and information messages
	-	Physical activities are consistent with verbal communication
Military Forces:		
	-	Alert posturing of military forces
	-	Location and maneuver of offensive forces and equipment
	-	Increased activity of military leadership and logistic forces
	-	Defensive posturing and preparations

Table 2 – Critical Information Indicators

Assessments using the indicators should guide future deterrence operations. Additionally, leaders and planners must consider second and third order effects as the result of U.S. deterrence activities. As highlighted in Chapter 3, U.S. trade embargos and an unwavering political policy provoked Japan to attack the United States and later prolonged the war. Changing deterrence strategy will not have an immediate effect on the adversary decision maker but over time properly focused deterrence activities can succeed as evident by the U.S. deterrence activities against Libya.

While deterrence measures of effectiveness are not readily available as to why an adversary did or did not take a desired action, planners can use intelligence indicators to determine indirectly if deterrence activities and messages achieved the desired outcome. Analysis of the adversary's public statements, rhetoric and military posturing, along with an understanding of the economic situation, alliances and the decision maker's motivation, can provide insight that the current deterrence activities are not achieving the desired outcome. Optimally, U.S. leaders will have time to adjust the deterrence approach to prevent a crisis situation from developing and ultimately to prevent conflict.

CHAPTER 6
RECOMMENDATIONS

The National Security Strategy states, "We are strengthening our military to…prevent and deter threats against the United States, its interests, and our allies and partners."[1] In addition to military actions, the document identifies a whole of government approach as necessary to succeed. Yet, the United States does not effectively implement deterrence strategy across government departments at the highest levels. The following recommendations require further development outside the scope of this paper but will improve national deterrence strategy.

Develop Deterrence Doctrine: Doctrine provides guiding principles for executing operations, yet a search for deterrence doctrine revealed that joint deterrence doctrine does not exist. The Joint Staff must develop joint deterrence doctrine with a level of specificity similar to the detail contained in military deception doctrine. The doctrine document should emphasize the focus of a deterrence plan and the importance of determining who is being deterred, who the key influencers are, and the conduits to influence the decision maker. The doctrine document should also include the requirement to develop a deterrence objective that indicates the specific action the adversary should or should not take. Additionally, deterrence doctrine must highlight the importance of influencing the adversary decision maker before the decision maker commits to taking the undesired act.

Furthermore, doctrine should emphasize the long lead time required to plan, execute and assess deterrence activities. The adversary decision maker must have enough time to

---

[1] U.S. President, *National Security Strategy* (Washington DC: Government Printing Office, May 2010), 14.

detect and analyze the activities and messages and then respond. Also U.S. Government personnel must have time to assess the effectiveness and adjust deterrence strategy before crisis develops.

Finally, deterrence doctrine should address the relationship and integration of deterrence activities and messages with other U.S. government agency's dissuasion efforts to achieve a common end state. In addition to including this concept in joint doctrine, United States Strategic Command must modify the DO JOC to address how military operations support Department of State negotiations with adversaries to encourage adversary restraint.

Develop Better Deterrence Strategy: The limited guidance contained in the Deterrence Operations Joint Operating Concept (DO JOC) highlights the importance of identifying the adversary decision maker and what action the adversary should or should not take. Yet the observations from deterrence strategy evolution and a review of current deterrence strategy indicate the current strategies are inadequate. The strategy documents make general statements about deterring attacks against the U.S. homeland and its allies.

To improve deterrence strategies, the strategy must identify specific adversary decision makers to influence and articulate the desired action or inaction that the adversary decision maker should or should not take. While the United States cannot specifically target every adversary decision maker, it is recommended that each Geographic Combatant Commander, in coordination with the Department of State, determine and focus deterrence efforts on two or three key decision makers within their geographic area of responsibility. Then planners should develop objectives and assess what the adversary decision maker concluded from friendly deterrence activities. When assessing the adversary's response to deterrence activities, leaders, planners and analysts must consider the data as presented and not insert mirror-imaging prejudices. This will allow leaders to objectively determine the adversary's intent and adjust the deterrence strategy as required.

Create an Organization to Synchronize Deterrence Activities: Effective deterrence operations require a whole of government approach. To achieve the desired end state, deterrence activities must be synchronized to focus efforts across all departments. Currently no single organization or document exists to accomplish the required synchronization. When national leadership establishes deterrence policy, each department implements its own strategy.

The Theater Campaign Plans coordinate with interagency organizations but cannot task agencies outside the Department of Defense. Additionally, other departments develop their own deterrence and dissuasion activities independent of the TCPs. For example, the multiple Department of State Mission Strategic Plans guide embassy personnel activities within a country. While the Department of State shares these plans with Combatant Commanders, they cannot task the Combatant Commander to accomplish military related activities such as military-to-military exchanges to strengthen or achieve a Department of State objective.

The National Security Council should establish an organization to coordinate and synchronize deterrence messages and activities across U.S. Government Departments. The organization should meet periodically to review past, current and future deterrence activities. Additionally, the organization should assess the adversary's response to past deterrence activities and adjust the deterrence strategy approach as required. This governing organization can use the synchronization matrix in Chapter 4, Table 1 to assist in monitoring activities of each department. Similar to the Policy Coordinating Committee's Counterterrorism Communication Center that primarily develops messages and strategies to discredit terrorist and their ideology, the organization should select one or two countries to develop and implement a detailed and focused deterrence strategy.

Develop Better Focus Indicators: Historically, adversary activities indicated that deterrence activities were failing, but for various reasons, U.S. leadership did not adjust its deterrence strategy which ultimately resulted in a crisis or conflict. Additionally, military activities alone do not deter aggression; therefore, military leaders, planners and intelligence analysts must expand their collection of adversary information. Planners and analysts already collect information on adversary military forces but must collect information from the five additional categories: political indicators, alliances, economic considerations, understanding motivation and communications. Developing appropriate PIRs focused on the six categories of indicators can assist in determining effectiveness of deterrence activities and messages. Intelligence analysts can provide operational and analytical feedback that report if the adversary decision maker received the deterrence message and what the adversary's reaction has been. Chapter 4 Table 1 contains example questions to assist in determining the adversary's response to deterrence activities.

CONCLUSION

The Capstone Concept for Joint Operations lists deterring potential adversaries as one of five national security challenges. The document further identifies "developing better ways to measure the effectiveness of deterrence efforts as a vital requirement."[1] Since the adversary decision maker will not readily admit to being deterred, planners must use indirect feedback to assess the effectiveness of deterrence activities. Properly developed priority intelligence requirements (PIR) can assist planners in determining if deterrence operations are achieving the desired end state.

Planners can develop alternative measures of effectiveness (MOE) by examining the six categories of historical indicators: political indicators, alliances, economic considerations, understanding motivation, communication and military forces. PIRs focused on these six categories provide operational and analytical feedback. Operational feedback determines if the adversary decision maker's information conduits observed or received the deterrence message. Analytical feedback determines the adversary decision maker's response to U.S. deterrence activities. Over time, data from the PIRs can provide insight into how the adversary will respond to future deterrence efforts.

To assist planners in developing better MOEs, U.S. leaders must develop better deterrence strategies. The United States has developed and publicized general deterrence strategies that do not employ the steps specified in the limited deterrence guidance contained in the Deterrence Operations Joint Operating Concept (DO JOC). Specifically, the strategies do not identify the leaders, decision makers or influencers the United States wants to deter, nor do they identify specific actions the adversary should or should not

---

[1] U.S. Joint Chiefs of Staff, *Capstone Concept*, 9-10.

take besides deter attacks against the United States or its allies. The vagueness of these strategies makes it difficult to determine if deterrence activities had the desired effect on an unknown adversary decision maker.

The United States continues to develop and publish general deterrence strategies but the strategies have evolved from having only a military force focus to implementing all instruments of national power through deterrent options. Integrating and synchronizing deterrence activities and messages across departments is problematic. Therefore, the National Security Council should establish an organization to oversee all U.S. Government deterrence activities. The organization should first focus on synchronizing deterrence activities toward two or three adversary decision makers. Once departments start executing various deterrence operations, the organization should meet periodically to assess the success or failure to influence the adversary decision maker and adjust and plan future activities as required.

Planners should apply guiding principles contained in doctrine when planning deterrence activities, yet a search for deterrence doctrine revealed that joint deterrence doctrine does not exist. The Joint Staff must develop joint deterrence doctrine with a level of specificity similar to the detail contained in military deception doctrine. The document should emphasize the importance of identifying the specific adversary decision maker to be deterred and what action the adversary is being deterred from taking. Additionally, the doctrine document should emphasize the long lead time required to plan, execute and assess deterrence activities.

While deterrence measures of effectiveness are not readily available as to why an adversary did or did not take a desired action, planners can use intelligence indicators to determine indirectly if deterrence activities and messages are or are not achieving the desired outcome. Analysis of the adversary's public statements, rhetoric and military posturing along with an understanding of the economic situation, alliances and the decision maker's motivation can provide insight that the current deterrence activities are not achieving the desired outcome. Optimally, U.S. leaders have enough time to adjust the deterrence approach in order to prevent conflict or allowing a crisis situation to develop.

APPENDIX 1
FLEXIBLE DETERRENT OPTIONS

Diplomatic
Alert and introduce special teams (e.g., public diplomacy)
Reduce international diplomatic ties
Increase cultural group pressure
Promote democratic elections
Initiate noncombatant evacuation procedures
Identify the steps to peaceful resolution
Restrict activities of diplomatic missions
Prepare to withdraw or withdraw U.S. embassy personnel
Take actions to gain support of allies and friends
Restrict travel of U.S. citizens
Gain support through the United Nations
Demonstrate international resolve

Information
Promote U.S. policy objectives through public policy statements
Ensure consistency of strategic communications themes and messages
Encourage Congressional support
Gain U.S. and international public confidence and popular support
Maintain open dialogue with the news media
Keep selected issues as lead stories
Increase protection of friendly critical information structure
Impose sanctions on communications systems technology transfer
Implement psychological operations

Military
Increase readiness posture of in place forces
Upgrade alert status
Increase intelligence, surveillance, and reconnaissance
Initiate or increase show-of-force actions
Increase training and exercise activities
Maintain an open dialogue with the news media
Take steps to increase U.S. public support
Increase defense support to public diplomacy
Increase information operations
Deploy forces into or near the potential operational area
Increase active and passive protection measures
Ensure consistency of strategic communications messages

Economic
Freeze or seize real property in the United States where possible
Freeze monetary assets in the United States where possible
Freeze international assets where possible
Encourage U.S. and international financial institutions to restrict or terminate financial   transactions
Encourage U.S. and international corporations to restrict transactions
Embargo goods and services
Enact trade sanctions
Enact restrictions on technology transfer
Cancel or restrict U.S.-funded programs
Reduce security assistance programs

Source: Data adapted from U.S. Joint Chiefs of Staff, *Joint Publication 5-0: Joint Operation Planning* (Washington DC: Government Printing Office, December 2006), A-2 – A-5. This table was compiled from Figures A-1 through A-4

LIST OF ACRONYMS USED

DO JOC – Deterrence Operations Joint Operating Concept

GCC – Global Combatant Commander

MOE – Measure of Effectiveness

MOP – Measure of Performance

NATO – North Atlantic Treaty Organization

NSS – National Security Strategy

OPEC – Organization of Petroleum Exporting Countries

PCC – Policy Coordinating Committee

PIR – Priority Intelligence Requirement

QDR – Quadrennial Defense Review

TCP – Theater Campaign Plan

U.A.E. – United Arab Emirates

U.S.S.R. – Union of Soviet Socialist Republics

WMD – Weapons of Mass Destruction

BIBLIOGRAPHY

Adams, Sam. *War of Numbers: An Intelligence Memoir.* South Royalton: Steerforth Press, 1994.

Betts, Richard. *Surprise Attack: Lessons for Defense Planning.* Washington DC: The Brookings Institution, 1982.

Brodie, Bernard, ed. *The Absolute Weapon: Atomic Power and World Order* . New York: Harcourt, Brace and Company, 1946.

Brodie, Bernard, ed. *The Future of Deterrence in U.S. Strategy.* Los Angeles: University of California, 1968.

Butow, Robert. *Japan's Decision to Surrender.* Stanford: Stanford University Press, 1954.

Chairman, Defense Science Board. *Report of the Defense Science Board Task Force on Nuclear Deterrence Skills.* Washington DC: U.S. Government Printing Office, September 2008.

Commadant of the Marine Corps, Chief of Naval Operations, and Commandant of the Coast Guard. *Naval Operations Concept: Implementing the Maritime Strategy.* Washington D.C.: Government Printing Office, 2010.

Commander, U.S. Africa Command. *United States Africa Command Theater Campaign Plan 7000-10.* Stuggart: Commander, U.S. Africa Command, October 2009.

Commander, U.S. European Command. *Headquarter United States European Command Theater Campaign Plan 2010.* Stuttgart: Director of Policy, Strategy, Partnering, and Capabilities, January 2010.

Commander, U.S. Joint Forces Command. *Commander's Handbook for Joint Battle Damage Assessment* . Washington DC: U.S. Government Printing Office, June 2004.

Commander, U.S. Strategic Command. *Deterrence Operations Joint Operating Concept Version 2.0.* Omaha, NE: United States Strategic Command, 2006.

—. *United States Strategic Command USSTRATCOM OPLAN 8010-08, Strategic Deterrence and Global Strike.* Offutt: Director, Plans and Policy, December 2008.

Davis, Brian. *Qaddafi, Terrorism, and the Origins of the U.S. Attack on Libya.* New York: Praeger Publishers, 1990.

Freedman, Lawrence. *The Evolution of Nuclear Strategy.* New York: St. Martin's Press, 1989.

George, Alexander, and Richard Smoke. *Deterrence in American Foreign Policy: Theory and Practice.* New York: Columbia University Press, 1974.

Gerard, Phillip. *Secret Soldiers.* New York: Dutton, 2002.

Gould-Davies, Nigel. "Rethinking the Role of Ideology in International Politics During the Cold War." *Journal of Cold War Studies*, 1, no 1 (Winter 1999): 90-109.

Grabo, Cynthia. *Anticipating Surprise: Analysis for Strategic Warning.* Washington, DC: Joint Military Intelligence College's Center for Strategic Intelligence Research, 2002.

Gray, Collin. *Maintaining Effective Deterrence.* Carlisle: Strategic Studies Institute, August 2003.

Hasegawa, Tsuyoshi. *Racing the Enemy: Stalin, Truman, and the Surrender of Japan.* Cambridge: The Belknap Press of Harvard University Press, 2005.

Huth, Paul and Bruce Russett. "What Makes Deterrence Work? Cases from 1900 to 1980." *World Politics*, 36 (July 1984): 496-526.

Hybel, Alex. *Power Over Rationality: The Bush Administration and the Gulf Crisis.* New York: State University of New York Press, 1993.

Jentelson, Bruce and Christopher Whytock. "Who "Won" Libya? The Force-Diplomacy Debate and Its Implications for Theory and Policy." *International Security*, 30 no 3, (2003): 47-86.

John F. Kennedy Library. *White House Diary.* September 5, 1962. http://whd.jfklibrary.org/Diary/NYT/New%20York%20Times%20Chronology%20September%201962.htm (accessed March 14, 2011).

Kecskemeti, Paul. *Strategic Surrender: The Politics of Victory and Defeat.* Stanford: Stanford University Press, 1957.

Kissinger, Henry. *Diplomacy.* New York: Simon and Schuster, 1994.

Kneece, Jack. *Ghost Army of World War II.* Gretna: Pelican Publishing Company, Inc, 2001.

Latimer, Jon. *Deception in War.* Woodstock: The Overlook Press, 2001.

Lebow, Richard and Janice Stein. *We All Lost the Cold War.* Princeton: Princeton University Press, 1994.

—. *When Does Deterrence Succeed and How Do We Know?* Ottawa: Canadian Institute for International Peace and Security, 1990.

Lebow, Richard. *Nuclear Crisis Management: A Dangerous Illusion.* Ithaca: Cornell University Press, 1987.

Legault, Albert. *Deterrence and the Atlantic Alliance.* Translated by Archibald Day. Lindsay: John Deyell Limited, 1966.

Lloyd, Mark. *The Art of Military Deception.* London: Leo Cooper, 1997.

Mearsheimer, John. *Conventional Deterrence.* Ithaca: Cornell University Press, 1985.

Montagu, Ewen. *The Man Who Never Was.* Philadelphia: J.B. Lippincott Company, 1954.

Morgan, Patrick. *Deterrence Now.* Cambridge: Cambridge University Press, 2003.

Mure, David. *Master of Deception: Tangled Webs in London and the Middle East.* London: William Kimber and Company Limited, 1980.

Naroll, Raoul, Vern Bullough, and Frada Naroll. *Military Deterrence in History: A Pilot Cross-Historical Survey.* Albany: State University of New York Press, 1974.

North Atlantic Treaty Organization Secretary General. *NATO Handbook.* Brussels: NATO Public Diplomacy Division, 2006.

Office of the Secretary of Defense. *Report of the Secretary of Defense Task Force on DoD Nuclear Weapons Management.* Washington DC: Secretary of Defense, 2008.

—. *Report of the Secretary of Defense Task Force on DoD Nuclear Weapons Managment Phase II.* Washington DC: Secretary of Defense, December 2008.

Organski, A.F.K. and Jacek Kugler. *The War Ledger.* Chicago: University of Chicago Press, 1980.

Parker, Geoffrey ed. *Cambridge Illustrated History of Warfare: The Triumph of the West.* New York: Cambridge University Press, 2000.

Payne, Keith. *The Fallacies of Cold War Deterrence and a New Direction.* Lexington: University Press of Kentucky, 2001.

Post, Jerrold. *Leaders and Their Followers in a Dangerous World: The Psychology of Political Behavior.* Ithaca: Cornell University Press, 2004.

Schaub Jr., Gary. "When is Deterrence Necessary? Gauging Adversary Intent." *Strategic Studies Quarterly,* (Winter 2009): 49-74.

Sifry, Micah and Christopher Cerf, eds. *The Gulf War Reader: History, Documents, Opinions.* New York: Time Books, 1991.

Sorley, Lewis. *Thunderbolt: General Creighton Abrams and the Army of His Times.* New York: Simon and Schuster, 1992.

Spitzer, Dean. *Transforming Performance Measurement: Rethinking the Way We Measure and Drive Organizational Success.* New York: AMACON Books, 2007.

Stanik, Joseph. *El Dorado Canyon: Reagan's Undeclared War with Qaddafi.* Annapolis: Naval Institute Press, 2003.

Steinbruner, John. "Beyond Rational Deterrence: A Struggle for New Conceptions." *World Politics*, 28, no 2 (January 1976): 223-245.

Stoessinger, John. *Why Nations Go To War.* Boston: Bedford/St. Martin's, 2001.

The American Presidency Project, *George Bush: Statement by Press Secretary Fitzwater on President Bush's Letter to President Saddam Huessin of Iraq*, January 12, 1991. http://www.presidency.ucsb.edu/ws/index.php?pid=19214&st=&st1=#axzz1OJnqVy Ou (accessed September 6, 2010).

The Home Office and the Air Ministry. *The Effects of the Atomic Bombs at Hiroshima and Nagasaki: Report of the British Mission to Japan.* London: His Majesty's Stationery Office, 1946.

Tzu, Sun. *The Art of War.* New York: Oxford University Press, 1971.

U.S. Air Force. *United States Air Force Posture Statement.* Washington DC: Department of the Air Force, February 2010.

U.S. Department of Defense. *National Defense Strategy of the United States of America.* Washington DC: U.S. Government Printing Office, March 2005.

—. *Quadrennial Defense Review Report.* Washington DC: Government Printing Office, February 2010.

—. *Strategy for Homeland Defense and Civil Support.* Washington DC: U.S. Government Printing Office, June 2005.

U.S. Department of State. *Diplomacy: The U.S. Department of State at Work.* Washington DC: U.S. Government Printing Office, June 2008.

—. U.S. Agency for International Development. *Strategic Plan: Fiscal Years 2007 - 2012.* Washington DC: Government Printing Office, May 2007.

—. Undersecretary for Public Diplomacy and Public Affairs. *U.S. National Strategy for Public Diplomcy and Strategic Communication.* Washington DC: Government Printing Office, May 2007.

U.S. Joint Chiefs of Staff. *Capstone Concept for Joint Operations, Version 3.0.* Washington DC: Government Printing Office, January 2009.

—. *Joint Doctrine, Education, & Training Electronic Information System, Joint Publications, Index.* https://jdeis.js.mil/jdeis/index.jsp?pindex=2 (accessed April 4, 2011).

—. *Joint Publication 1-02: Department of Defense Dictionary of Military and Associated Terms.* Washington DC: Government Printing Office, September 2010.

—. *Joint Publication 2-0: Joint Intelligence.* Washington DC: U.S. Government Printing Office, June 2007.

—. *Joint Publication 3-0: Joint Operations, Change 2.* Washington DC: Government Printing Office, March 2010.

—. *Joint Publication 3-13.4: Military Deception.* Washington DC: Government Printing Office, July 2006.

—. *Joint Publication 3-13: Information Operations.* Washington DC: Government Printing Office, February 2006.

—. *Joint Publication 5-0: Joint Operation Planning.* Washington DC: U.S. Government Printing Office, December 2006.

—. *Unified Command Plan.* Washington DC: Government Printing Office, April 2011.

U.S. President. *National Security Strategy.* Washington DC: Government Printing Office, May 2010.

U.S. Secretary of the Air Force. *Air Force Doctrine Document 2-1.5: Nuclear Operations.* Washington DC: U.S. Government Printing Office, July 1998.

—. *Air Force Doctrine Document 3-72: Nuclear Operations.* Washington DC: Government Printing Officer, June 2007.

—. *Air Force Doctrine Document 3-72: Nuclear Operations, Change 1.* Washington DC: U.S. Government Printing Office, September 2010.

United Nations. *Security Council Resolutions - 1991: Resolution 678: Iraq-Kuwait.* 29 November 1991. http://daccess-dds-ny.un.org/doc/RESOLUTION/GEN/NR0/575/28/IMG/NR057528.pdf?OpenElement (accessed March 9, 2011).

—. *Security Council Resolutions - 1993: Resolution 883: Libyan Arab Jamahiriya.* 11 November 1993. http://daccess-dds-ny.un.org/doc/UNDOC/GEN/N93/626/78/PDF/N9362678.pdf?OpenElement (accessed March 9, 2011).

Whiteneck, Daniel and Michael Gerson. *Deterrence and Influence: The Navy's Role in Preventing War.* Open-file, Center for Naval Analysis, Alexandria VA: US Navy Department, 2009.

Wohlforth, William. "A Certain Idea of Science: How International Relations Theory Avoids the New Cold War History." *Journal of Cold War Studies*, 1, no. 2 (Spring 1999): 39-60.

Woods, Kevin. *The Iraqi Perspectives Report: Saddam's Senior Leadership on Operation Iraqi Freedom from the Official U.S. Joint Forces Command Report.* Annapolis: Naval Institute Press, 2006.

Woodward, Bob. *The Commanders.* New York: Simon and Schuster, 2002.

VITA

Lieutenant Colonel Rose enlisted in the Air Force in 1982. After serving eight years in a variety of maintenance and contracting positions she received her commission through the Air Force Officer Training School graduating with Distinction. Colonel Rose earned a Master of Science Degree in Management with Computer Science Application from Lesley University, Cambridge Massachusetts. She is currently a student at the Joint Advanced Warfighting School, Joint Forces Staff College and will earn a Master of Science degree in Joint Campaign Planning and Strategy summer 2011.

Lieutenant Colonel Rose has over twenty years experience in space and missile operations. She operated the Minuteman III Intercontinental Ballistic Missile System using two different operating systems. Lieutenant Colonel Rose earned instructor and evaluator qualifications and was the Chief, Weapons and Tactics Flight. Most recently she commanded the 741st Missile Squadron, Minot Air Force Base, North Dakota. In this capacity she ensured the safe, secure and reliable operation of five Launch Control Centers and 50 Intercontinental Ballistic Missiles.

In the field of space operations, Lieutenant Colonel Rose operated the Defense Support Program ground station and the Space Based Infrared System. Both systems provide missile warning and technical intelligence data to Combatant Commanders and National Leadership supporting the defense of the United States and its allies. She earned instructor and evaluator qualifications and was recognized as the Best Space Operations Crew and Best Missile Warning Crew in Air Force Space Command, 1997. Lieutenant Colonel Rose served as the Operations Officer for the Space Based Infrared System.

In her staff officer positions, Lieutenant Colonel Rose earned Air Force level recognition as the Air Force Military Deception Officer of the Year 2000 and the Air Force Military Deception Program Manager of the Year 2001. She provided information operations planning support to Operation ENDURING FREEDOM and Operation NOBLE EAGLE. Furthermore, she served at United States Strategic Command representing and advocating Joint Forces Component Commander for Space initiatives.

www.ingramcontent.com/pod-product-compliance
Lightning Source LLC
Chambersburg PA
CBHW080323290526
45790CB00005B/2154